Coaching Girls Ponytail Softball

Coaching Girls Ponytail Softball

Danford Chamness

Writers Club Press
New York Lincoln Shanghai

Coaching Girls Ponytail Softball

Writers Club Press
an imprint of iUniverse, Inc.

For information address:
iUniverse
2021 Pine Lake Road, Suite 100
Lincoln, NE 68512
www.iuniverse.com

ISBN: 0-595-24179-4

Printed in the United States of America

To Amanda, Hannah, Ilene, Jenny, Ravyn, Larry, Scott, Bill, Bob and David for this wonderful adventure.

Contents

Foreword

This book was written expressly for you who are coaching children in Softball. We stress how to teach children this fun game and to have fun doing it. The book covers all facets of the game from "how to" throwing to strategies and tactics.

When coaching children it should be a fun experience for everyone, for you, for the parents, and most important of all, for the children. As a coach, we cover the teaching attitude and methods. We always keep in mind that these are children, and the game is for the kids and not for the adults. Winning isn't everything, but learning to play well and wanting to win is.

We have taken the children from first grade through the eighth grade and broken them into four categories. In each category we discuss the players needs and abilities, what they are capable of in both the physical and emotional sense, and their limitations. We have also defined the coach's role, the parent's role and the player's role.

We primarily stress how to teach children this complex game and to have fun doing it. Understand that the team is a composite of three important elements. The coaching staff, the parents and the players of the team. Leadership of this composite rests upon the coaching staff. It has the responsibility for directing and maintaining the program from its beginning until its end.

As a coach you are building attitudes and memories with these youngsters which they will carry with them for a lifetime. You are the first to give them an identity away from home or school. You have made them a member of a team, and assigned them a responsible position on the team.

This is their first step to independence and self reliance. And you are helping them take that first step. Leading a youngster into their own identity is the birth of their character to come. There is not enough praise that can be given to you for your selfless efforts to train these young people.

Always remain aware that these kids are the hope of all of our tomorrow's. And by doing a good job with them early, you have given more to their future than you realize.

Thank you for your participation.

Acknowledgments

The "National Youth Sports Coaches Association" was developed to train coaches in the techniques and methods of coaching young people. It is coaching specific. I am proud to be a member of this organization, and I highly recommend that you consider becoming one yourself.

NYSCA

National Youth Sports Coaching Association
2050 Vista Parkway, West Palm Beach, FL 33411
(561) 684-1141, (800) 729-2057, Fax (561) 684-2546
E-Mail: nays @ nays.org
Web Site: Intp:/www.nays.org

Becoming a NYSCA certified coach does not indicate that you are qualified in the sense of a paid coach on the high school, college, or professional level. By virtue of your attending the NYSCA Training Certification Program conducted by a qualified Clinician. NYSCA Headquarters certifies that you have been trained in your responsibilities to children in sports specifically.

The City of Burbank, Parks and Recreation Sports Department is an outstanding example of what a well organized group can do. I have had the good fortune of working as a volunteer coach for this department for a number of years. With limited facilities and multiple sports in progress at any one time, they perform pure magic when it comes to scheduling games and practice sessions.

The city through it's meticulous selection of staffing personnel has managed to attract an outstanding number of dedicated people. I thank them for all of the support they have given to the coaches in the coaches efforts to train the children in this community.

Chapter 1

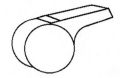

Coaches Corner

So you're ready to coach? Great! This book is dedicated to you and the member's of your team. And as a coach you are more than just a trainer of young athletes in the fine art of this chosen sport, but their mentor and teacher. This carries a lot of responsibility. Not just the idea of building a winning team, but the molding of character and creating a firm foundation of good sportsmanship.

As their coach, you are responsible for scheduling all practices, getting uniforms, setting game dates, handling the players rotation roster, first aid on the court, player releases and a hundred other details. How well you organize your program is important. You must also have the most current rules publication available to you because almost every year, some rule changes.

The adventure of coaching Ponytail softball will bring delights that you may never have known. Girl athletes are great. This carries a lot of responsibility. Not just the idea of building a winning team, but the molding of character and creating a firm foundation of good sportsmanship. Learn to laugh at yourself and laugh with your team.

Your own goal should be to have fun teaching these youngsters how to play this most popular of all sports. Make it a point to bring your sense of humor to every practice session or game. The game is based on only four individual physical attributes and they are throwing, catching, batting and running.

As the coach, you also become the team's trainer. The Training side is when you are teaching the fundamental skills required to play the game, it's the "how to" phase. This phase does not include practice games, it is specifically training. Under training, you will run practice drills, and give instructions which assist the player in learning "how to". Depending on the age and experience of your new team, the amount of "how to" may vary considerably.

Training for the younger players will require more training time in the basic fundamentals than the older girls. You assess the skill level early on with your team by having them perform the most basic skills required to play the game. Once the teams basic skill level is determined, you either raise or lower the basic skill level of drills to be practiced.

At this point you must develop realistic goals you should hope to achieve with the players. Create a schedule of how and when you should reach a particular goal. Once an overall plan is put together, you are organized. Now you have a means of measuring yourself and your teams success. Having a reference point for achievement is as important to you as it is to the team.

Making your training time count is based upon how you prepare the training program and the amount of detail you put into it. Always have a plan in advance, then follow it. Those youngsters who are slower to develop skills than the others will of course require more of your personal attention. Give it with a smile.

You must also remain aware that safety in practice sessions is a big consideration. Restrict swinging the bat practices until they can be supervised. Head and face injuries are nasty problems for everyone. Also remember that there is one fear that lingers with all girls on your team, and that is getting hammered by the ball.

In Pitch-T and straight pitch softball, the two players most likely to receive an injury are the Batter and the Pitcher. In T-Ball it is the Pitcher who is most apt to be injured by a batted ball. Reaction times for youngsters is slower than for the older players. Next on the list of injured are the infielders from "hot" ground balls. A bad bounce can jump into a kids face.

When we are coaching youngsters, consider girls from 6 to 14 as being in this category. They arrive filled with hope and expectation to improve their skills and to have fun. Don't forget the word play in "play ball". Leave the furrowed brow, pulled down mouth and scornful voice at the door.

You are the leader, trainer, booster, supporter, manager, and a host of many positive things. To be all of that requires constant monitoring of yourself and your reactions. It's a darn tough job. All of us have reflex reactions that at times can be very inappropriate to a situation at hand. Often times holding these in check is difficult if not almost impossible.

Reflex is a conditioned response which can cause us to say or do something we will later regret. Some people call this overreaction, and it is. That old business about counting to ten first, really holds true, so use it. Like it or not, you are the authority figure. Always conduct yourself as such. Don't smoke, use smokeless tobacco or profanity in front of the team.

Now is a good time to consider whether or not you're coaching your own daughter. If that is the case, there are some guidelines you must consider. Consider first if your child wants you to be her coach. Some children do not want to be coached by a parent because the relationship is to close to their daily routine.

Next, review your own reasons and interest for coaching your child. Are you attempting to make her a "star" by giving the child preferential treatment? If that be the case, you're off on the wrong foot. That causes a lot of conflict among other the players on the team, and with their parents. Your daughter is then subjected to a negative backlash from the other players.

Another problem we run into when coaching our own children is we sometimes expect more from them than their counterparts. This is unfair to the child. Let the child grow at her own rate. Allow her the freedom of being like any other kid on the team. Do not compare your child's accomplishments to those of others. Try to keep the playing field level for all participants.

Let's talk about the kids for a moment. They are pretty much blank pages for you. They come in a variety of sizes, maturity levels, skill levels, and of playing experience. Some have good hand—eye coordination and some don't. Some may have physical disabilities such as asthma, epilepsy, shortness of breath, hard of hearing, or eye problems which are not obvious by looking at them.

Take any age group, for instance 10 to 11 year old girls, their abilities and sizes will run the gambit. However, there are several common denominators among all youngsters. Their vulnerability, their wanting to please you, and their need for positive reinforcement. Simple achievements build their self esteem. They need you to be their positive booster.

If your kids are lucky, you will create a sports sanctuary where they learn to play the game and have fun. Having fun is the key to good coaching. Make it fun for the players and yourself. Consider that you know nothing about their outside environment or inner family relationships. Young people have many stressful conditions imposed on them by family expectations, school and their own social group.

You have no way of knowing what goes on where and with whom in your charge. Child abuse can be anything from indifference and neglect to murder. Harsh words but true. It exists on a wide variety of levels and you as a coach should be aware of it. Take for instance the act of expressing your delight over a players successful performance on the court.

High five's, shoulder slaps, hair ruffling or shoulder squeezes are affectionate displays of caring and approval. And these have a place in the sports arena, they demonstrate acceptance and improve self worth.

However, never, and I repeat never pat, rub or touch the kids below the belt. This can easily be misunderstood by her and others.

A player expects fairness from the coach when playing schedules are assigned. No girl wants to sit on the bench while the others are in the game. Players then reflect upon themselves that you don't feel they are good enough to play. And they assume that you, without saying a word have shown your feelings about her playing ability. If she can recognize, and should, that you are being both fair to her as an individual and the team as a whole, you've got a happy camper.

An example of kids thinking can go like this: The girl had a great game, everything she did worked. It was the best she had ever played but the team lost the game. Because the team lost did not make her unhappy because she was happy with how she played. Conversely the girl played a terrible game, nothing worked that she tried but the team won. How do you think she felt about herself? She felt good because the team won.

Winning isn't everything. Losing isn't everything. Playing the game well and wanting to win is everything. Never make too much out of a game lost. Instead have the team see it as a learning experience, discuss what adjustments you as a team can make to improve your win/loss performance. Let the kids know that you are with them and behind them all the way. When you win, you all win, when you lose, you all lose.

Encourage the working relationship between the team and you as the coach. Keep an open mind on suggestions and ideas from your team. Let them participate in what the team is doing. Let the players arrive at your observation, then confirm it.

Coaching really starts when you begin practice games. Conduct your coaching during practice games in the same manner you will use during a league game. Coaches will refrain from verbally coaching their players in a negative manner while they are on the field. Discretion of the umpire or the Sports Office Staff will be used to handle the situation.

Here again is that philosophy of don't scold. A player may have made a poor choice in what she did, but scolding won't undo the mistake. Both you and the team must accept the reality that mistakes do happen, and they are okay. You simply emphasize what you would like to have done instead of what was done.

The more advanced and skilled your players or team becomes, the easier your job gets. When you are coaching a young team that is just developing it's skills, you are looking primarily at the basic mistakes the players are making. You begin listing in your mind the things you will have to emphasize in training.

This approach makes the team feel they are supported by you instead of scrutinized by you. Build from the positive things your players are doing well. Ring in the reins a little on the "must win" thinking. Direct the teams efforts and allow them to experiment and have fun. Having fun and bonding with their teammates will develop the winning team for you and them.

Every team you will coach, whether very young or young adult, will develop a bond among themselves. Their shared experience in working towards a common goal is a coalition of individuals. You will be watching this bond form as they share the playing experience.

One bonding method I use becomes our practice and game ritual when we are together as a team. After every practice and both before and after every game, we all form a circle with our hands touching inside and do a "on three", one, two, three, "YEAH TEAM!" Of course we call out our teams name as loudly as possible.

Once the bond has begun to take shape, you must consider more closely how you either correct or instruct your individual players. From within their bond, you are the outsider. Sure, you are the coach, but not a member of the team. Girls are like rope, you can lead them, pull them along, but you can't push them very well.

Coaching girls brings in a unique set of problems for a male coach. First, as a male, you don't possess any of the intuition for the female motto fini. Where you can accept group criticism as belonging only to the group, the girls personalize the criticism as if selected personally by you. Girls are tough and touchy. Patience and forethought will be required if criticism is to be made.

This is the very reason I avoid making a negative comment about how a player does or did something. Instead I tell them what I would like to see them do and suggest how to do it. Always build on the positive things your players do and forget about worrying over the negative things that were done.

You are the authority figure, there is a separateness you should maintain as an instructing coach. Always refer to the girls by their names which keeps everything on an even keel. They should refer to you as coach, or mister, or misses and not by your first name. We, as coaches must stand apart in order to get the response we want from them, for them.

During a game, limit comments to individual players about what they are doing or not doing while they are on the field. If you have a player who is not doing what you have requested of her, wait until the inning is over which allows her to come to the bench. Conduct your business with her privately and calmly.

If the team is not doing what you've asked them to do. Do corrections in a positive and reinforcing way. No scolding. Explain as clearly as possible the changes you are looking for and do it with a smile.

When you are coaching a team of good players. You don't have to look at basic performance mistakes, because they don't make them. You are now in the process of building teamwork. The longer a good team plays together as a team, the more proficient they become. At this coaching level you are teaching your team how to improve and implement strategies and tactics. Therefore during the game, you are looking for strategies and tactics to help them win.

How do you handle an unruly parent who is shouting at the players on the field during the game? If a parent is admonishing his own child, ask him to help the team by taking some of his extra time to work with his kid to improve her performance. Always try to enlist the parent in a positive way to gain the participation you want. Spectators may not verbally coach from the bleachers, sidelines, opposite side of the field, or in any way interfere with the game. Managers are responsible for the conduct of their spectators and for informing parents on the rules and philosophy of the program.

For some unknown reason, some parents get out of control as spectators. Some parents seem to feel they know more about the game than anyone else. They will boo the officials call and argue from the stands. Some will begin to instruct the officials as to fouls which should be called and aren't. It doesn't end there.

After a game, you may have someone call you at home and chew on your ear for some mistake a player made, and it's your fault. The kid would be better off in another position, not the one she is playing. You are going to hear it all. Everyone is your critic. Don't allow those people to undermine your efforts. You aren't doing this for them, you are doing it for the players, and remind yourself of that.

Now that you are the coach, let's look at what this entails other than being the teams trainer and provider. You should keep a first aid kit available at all times during practice and games. Ice packs are almost always in demand for bangs and bruises, with Band-Aid running a close second.

A coach is responsible;
For teaching the fundamentals of the game.
For creating a good learning environment.
For treating each child fairly.
For individual training needs.
For each child's personal safety.
For each child's safety from others abuse.
For setting a good example.
For creating a team environment.
For building players self esteem.
For encouragement and player fun.
For having patience with the children.

For the parents behavior during a game.
For the players behavior during a game.

A coach has the right;

To cooperation from the parents.
To cooperation from the player.
To cooperation from the league.
To bench a player for inappropriate behavior.
To suspend a player from play.
To not accept a problem player on the team.
To assign his players to their positions.
To have adequate practice facilities.
To fairness in scheduling with the league.

One last note, during a league game or when a number of people are in attendance, only allow your team to use the restrooms when all of the players go together. Keep them together at all times for their own individual safety. Make sure all players are picked up after the game or practice and never leave one behind alone. If you have a player who is waiting for someone to pick them up, you wait with them.

Language of the Game

Below are listed the most commonly used terms in softball and you should begin early with the youngsters to use them. Vernacular is important to the players and how they converse with each other in their own sports language.

Balk—An illegal motion by the pitcher resulting in a ball being credited to the batter and runners advancing one base.

Baserunner—An offensive player who is either on base or attempting to reach a base.

Batter's box—Rectangles on either side of home plate designating the area in which a batter must stand.

Bench—Where the players sit in the dugout when not on the field.

Bunt—A hitting method accomplished by holding the bat in such a way as the ball is hit softly into the infield near home plate.

Change-up—Using the same motions as to throw a fast ball, the pitcher throws a slow ball to deceive the batter.

Choke up—Or choking up, is moving the grip on the bat away from the knob end toward the bat head.

Curveball—A pitch thrown with spin to cause the ball to curve away from the expected course of flight. It is usually thrown down and to the left when thrown by a right handed pitcher with just the reverse when thrown by a left handed pitcher.

Double—A hit that allows the batter to reach second base safely.

Double play—A play by the defense which results in two baserunners being put out.

Dugout—A caged section separating the players from the spectators and adjacent to the playing field away from home plate. It is where the player bench is housed.

Error—A mistake made by defense that allows a runner to advance to a base safely, whereas that player would otherwise been unable to advance or have been put out.

Fair territory—The area of the playing field between the foul lines.

Fastball—A high speed pitch which may rise slightly as it comes to home plate.

Fielders choice—A situation allowing a batter to reach first base safely because the fielder decided to put a different baserunner out.

Fly ball—Usually a ball that is hit high in the air.

Fly-out—A fly ball that is caught, resulting in the batter being out.

Forced out—An out caused by the ball reaching a base before the runner who had no choice but to advance. An example is the play where the ball is thrown to second base instead of first to put the baserunner out who was on first base and must advance to second base.

Foul ball—A batted ball that lands in or rolls into foul territory before passing first or third base.

Foul line—Either of two lines extending from home plate through the outer edges of first and third base to the outfield boundaries.

Foul territory—The area of territory that lies outside the foul line boundaries.

Grand Slam—When the batting team has runners on all three bases and the batter hits the ball well enough to bring in all baserunners and reach home plate safely.

Ground ball or grounder—A batted ball that bounces or rolls along the ground in the infield.

Groundout—A ground ball fielded by an infielder which results in the batter being put out.

Home Run—When a batter has hit a ball well enough to allow him to run all bases and return to home plate safely.

Home Team—Occupies the bench on the third base side of the field.

Infield—The area of the playing field enclosed by the bases and home plate.

Inning—A division of the game which allows each team to have a turn at bat.

Lead—A position taken by the baserunner off the base towards the next base baserunner wants to obtain. This is not allowed in softball.

Leadoff—The first batter in an inning.

Line drive—A ball hit by the batter that travels in a flat straight line through the infield.

Out—A player is called "out" and returned to his bench if he strikes out on three strikes, fly's out, is tagged by the ball when off base, or forced out. Three outs for a team ends their segment of the inning.

Outfield—That portion of the field outside the infield territory and between the foul lines.

Passed ball—A pitch not hit by the batter and missed by the catcher.

Pop fly—A ball hit high in the air and fielded inside the infield.

Retired Batter—A batter who has been struck out.

RBI's or runs batted in—A run driven in by a batter.

Run—A scoring unit credited to a team for each runner who crosses home plate safely.

Sacrifice—A bunt or fly ball which results in the batter being put out in order to advance a baserunner to the next base or bases.

Scoring position—When a player is on second or third base and could score on a base hit.

Single—A hit that allows the batter to reach first base safely.

Strikeout—A batter being put out after having three strikes

Strike zone—The area over home plate through which the ball must pass to be called a strike.

Tag—To touch.

Tag up—A baserunner remaining on base during a fly ball with the intention of advancing to the next base after the ball is caught.

Third Base—The last base a runner tags before going to home plate.

Triple—A ball so hit allowing the batter to reach third base safely.

Triple play—A defensive play that results in putting three players out.

Visiting Team—Occupies the bench on the first base side of the field.

Walk—A batter advancing to first base after receiving a fourth ball.

Wild Pitch—A pitch not hit by the batter and uncatchable by the catcher.

Wild Throw—A ball thrown by any player that is uncatchable by any other player.

Chapter 2

Players Bench

The youngsters coming into the baseball program want a place where they can play with others like themselves and practice whatever skills they have. Usually they arrive with a great deal of interest about the sport and an attitude about their own ability. However the majority of youngsters are shy and don't want to be singled out to do things which they may not do well.

However, they all want to fit in with the others in your program. Each player wants an opportunity to do what she does best, or thinks she does best. She expects the coach to recognize her skills and abilities and instruct her in how to improve them. She expects to be included in all of the activities fairly.

It is my opinion that every player believes that she or he can play any position on the team and expects the opportunity to do so. And they should be given that opportunity until they discover for themselves where they are most comfortable playing. Comfort will come from the success they have in a given assignment.

Players prior to the age of puberty are looking at the sport for fun. Players after reaching puberty look at the sport as a way to establish an identity. Young players share interest and involvement. Older players share the same interest and involvement but bring another dimension when seeking identity. In overall respect, all players are wanting to have fun with the game and all of them should.

All players regardless of age seek leadership from adults and coaches. All players want acceptance and recognition. All players want to play in the game. Some girls are seeking a haven away from their outside environment.

To find a place where they fit. A player expects fairness from the coach when playing schedules are assigned. No girl wants to sit on the bench while the others are in the game.

No player wants to either be made the subject of scrutiny nor to be ignored. During a practice or a game, she expects leadership from the coach in how to best play the game. She is more than willing to follow directions if they are explained in a way which she can understand. Most players feel that if they work hard in practice, do their best as directed, should have the right to play in the game.

This is a players fairness doctrine that should be adhered to. No player is looking to be the fair haired girl, and resents it if there appears to be someone else who is. Girls in the sport find their own place among their peers. It is a place of comfort for them to play from in the team.

No player on your team wants to be scolded, talked to abusively or harshly corrected for whatever mistake she makes. She does not expect to be ordered around like a small child or treated as if she's not good enough to be with the other players. All youngsters are sensitive to correction and how corrections are made.

Player's Rights & Responsibilities:
To fairness and respect.
To have fun learning and playing.
To not be ridiculed or harshly scolded.
To make mistakes without punishment.
To a fair amount of playing time in the game.
To encouragement for effort.
To protection from abuse by others.
To a safe environment.
A player is responsible;
For attending practices.
For attending the game.
For trying To make a learning effort.

For good conduct on the field.
For cooperating with others.
For following directions.
For letting the coach know if she is ill.
For staying with the team at all times.
For asking permission to leave the game.

Chapter 3

Parents Expectations

Parents expect their children to be taught how to play their game of choice while having fun. They expect the coach to be thoughtful, considerate, kind and fair to their prize possession. Parents who involve their young children in sports do so for a variety of reasons. First they want their children to have fun in sports, and group activities.

Parents want their youngsters to acquire self esteem and confidence and to learn the values of good sportsmanship. They want their kids to build a network of friends and enjoy an activity which in the future may guide them away from trouble. All of this is as it should be, and it is also the coach's focus as well.

Parents sometimes have unrealistic expectations about their child's ability to master the basics of the game. They often expect to much from their youngsters. These expectations should be tempered with the realization that they are only children. We have a situation where kids are playing at grown up games. Some children will develop quicker than others and some will be slower than the rest. So what! Parents must let the kids have their play time.

All parents want their children to perform well. When they don't, they get disappointed with their children, the team and the coaches. Not a good thing to have happen. They should never be unhappy over kids trying to play this game as best they can. When the parent gets unhappy with their child's, or the children's performance, their kid feels defeated by not living up to their expectations of her. This spoils it for the child.

Parents on a rotating basis will provide snacks and treats for the team to be distributed after the game. If the team consists of 15 players for instance, bring enough for at least twenty or more. What happens is very simple, most of the team members have sibling brothers or sisters who will want to share in the treats. Treats are usually a snacker such as potato chips, Fritos, Cheetos, etc. and a cold drink.

Normally after a game, the team is huddled with positive comments spread around to encourage the players. After the huddle, the providing parent will conduct the treats hand-out for the team.

Some things a parent should never do.

Never ridicule one of the team members lack of ability to play well to your child. By bad rapping another players deficiencies to your child, only makes her defensive about "her" team.

Never take your coach to task in front of the team. You may not know all you should about either playing the game or coaching it. Never assume that you know why a coach is doing what he is doing.

Never scold your child in the presence of the team either at a practice or a game for what you feel she did or did not do.

Never insist that your child should play if she is ill or suffering from an injury. No child should be requested to play if she is in pain. It could result in long term injury which we all wish to avoid.

During a game, never shout and demean another team and its players by completely forgetting that the other team is made of children the same as your own.

During a game, don't take the officials to task over a call or calls that he has made. It will not change the officials decision and only reflects upon your team and your child.

A parent has the right;

To share in their child's training experience.

To encourage their child and the team.

To be concerned about their child's safety.

To see their child treated fairly.

To want their child's self esteem to grow.

To expect the coach to teach sportsmanship.

To expect the coach to set a good example.

A parent has the responsibility;

To get their child to practice on time.

To get their child to the game on time.

To notify the coach of illness.

To participate with team activities.

A parent has the responsibility for picking up their child after a practice or a game. If that is not possible, then advise the coach of who will be recovering the player so the coach will know.

Chapter 4

Rostering a Team

The rules of the National Federation of High School Associations shall be enforced in the Hap Minor/Ponytail Leagues unless amended. Rules like the Southern California Municipal Athletic Federation shall be enforced in the Ponytail Leagues unless amended below.

I would like to suggest that you roster your team with children from the same grade level. Don't mix and match. If it's all first graders or all fourth graders that's fine. Human nature has a built in sorting machine that sets a pecking order. The nature of things can undermine your teams interrelationships between players and create a form of segregation.

This may not be voiced by your players to you, but it will be there working against you. Think about it, before you do it. At least attempt to have a homogenous team. Each player then is truly among her peers.

Roster Rules:

A roster must contain the name, address, city, phone number, signature, school, birthdate, and grade of each player.

1. Get a list of players from the Sports Office waiting list.
   a. If you have one player or a group, have them help find new players to join the team Never ask a child to quit her team to join yours. Names obtained from the Sports Office will be used first.
   b. We suggest coaches follow minimum/maximum guidelines set up in the rules for roster formation.

   c. If you want to pick up a team from a specific school, have the players do "scouting" for you. Be sure to check with the principal of the school before going onto the playground.

2. Pick up Manager information from the Sports Office and read all the material.

3. Contact the players and let them know they are on your team.

   a. Be sure to give them your name and phone number. Have them write it down.

   b. For younger players, give the information to the parents.

   c. Be sure to have them call you if they decide not to play.

   d. Let the Sports Office know if any child is not going to be on your team.

4. Call a meeting of all children and their parents.

   a. Advise them to bring money for the team entry fee (insurance, etc.) and team equipment if needed.

   b. Ask for parental help if needed or desired and choose an emergency manager in case you can't make it to a game. Get fathers and mothers to help coach the team if possible.

   c. Set up practice time convenient to you and your team.

   d. Most teams are commercially sponsored. Find out if any parent would be willing to sponsor or work for a company that would be willing to pick up the cost of sponsoring your team. It is a tax write-off for businesses that sponsor teams.

5. Pick a team name.

6. Decide on team uniform.

   a. Teams may choose what type of uniforms they want. Uniforms are not mandatory. However, most teams choose to have them.

   b. Everyone must have a glove subject to the regulations listed for equipment.

   c. Rubber cleats are allowed. Steel cleats are forbidden; the multi-purpose sport shoe is recommended.

7. Discuss philosophy of the league.

a. Discuss the Player Code of Conduct.

b. Discuss the player responsibility to the team.

c. Emphasize Sportsmanship.

d. In T-ball, this league is designed to be a learning recreational experience. The competitive aspect should be played down.

8. Purchase equipment.

a. Catcher's protective equipment.

b. Bats—Regulation Little League for Baseball. Regulation softball for beginning pitch or T-Ball/Ponytail Softball.

c. Balls. Check with the Sports Office for the type of ball required for your league.

Chapter 5

Managing A Team

The rules of the National Federation of High School Associations shall be enforced in the Hap Minor/Ponytail Leagues unless amended. Rules like the Southern California Municipal Athletic Federation shall be enforced in the Ponytail Leagues unless amended below.

All federations involved with youth baseball operates pretty much the same. We will adhere to the rules and regulations set forth by one of the nations premier municipal organizations with a long and successful career in bringing organized baseball and softball to the young people in their own community.

I. Manager's And Coach's Responsibility

A. All managers and coaches must be in good standing with the Burbank Athletic Federation.

B. Managers and Coaches shall be required to comply with the requirements established by the Park, Recreation and Community Services Department for background checks for volunteers.

C. Managers are directly responsible to the Burbank Athletic Federation and the Park, Recreation and Community Services Department for league fees, rosters, team eligibility, team business, and conduct of players, coaches, parents, and spectators.

D. Managers are responsible for proper care and immediate return of all Park, Recreation and Community Services equipment and all sponsor's equipment and uniforms.

E. Managers are responsible for ensuring the eligibility of all the players who participate for their team. **Penalty:** Suspension of illegal player, forfeiture of all games in which ineligible player played illegally and suspension of manager.

F. All teams must have an adult manager on the bench at all times during practices and games

G. The Manager, coaches and bat handler signatures must appear on the official team roster to be eligible to sit on the players' bench.

H. If a manager or coach is apt to be late, arrangements should be made for someone else to have the line-up and equipment, in order to start the game on time.

I. Only 2 coaches and 1 manager may be in the dugout at any given time. Any changes in this policy should be cleared with the field supervisor. Manager will be responsible for keeping unauthorized persons out of the dugout.

J. It is the managers responsibility to prevent players from leaving the field and mingling with the spectators during the game.

K. Managers will be responsible for keeping their teams off the general playing area until the end of the preceding game.

L. Managers are responsible for initiating Players' Medical Benefit Fund accident report forms (available in Sports Office) within 7 days of the accident.

M. Managers must report all accidents to the field supervisor at the time of the accident so that a Park, Recreation and Community Services Department accident form may be completed.

N. Coaches will refrain from verbally coaching their players in a negative manner while they are on the field. Discretion of the umpire or the Sports Office Staff will be used to handle the situation.

0. Spectators may not verbally coach from the bleachers, sidelines, opposite side of the field, or in any way interfere with the game.

P. Managers are responsible for the conduct of their spectators and for informing parents on the rules and philosophy of the program.

Q. Managers, coaches and players may not smoke in the dugout or on the playing field.

R. The selection to be an All-star manager or coach is an honor and privilege. It is not in the spirit of fair play to ask a member of an All-star team to quit her team to join yours.

Ponytail Softball Regulations
II. Players Eligibility

A. All players must be in good standing with the Burbank Athletic Federation.

B. A player is not eligible until her signature and her parents signature appears on a team's roster. **PENALTY** for using an ineligible player: **FORFEITURE** of all league games in which she played illegally, suspension of player and manager.

C. A player may not play in two leagues under the auspices of B.A.F. or on two teams in Burbank Park, Recreation and Community Services Department leagues at the same time during the season. CIF players are eligible upon completion of current school season. Girls have the option to play in either baseball or softball leagues, but not both. Boys may not play in the softball league. NOTE: No team may have more than 8 players who played Parochial League.

D. The following standards will be applied to the Ponytail classification procedure.

1. |Team grouping is determined by the highest grade represented by any girl on the team.
2. Girls may play above their grouping but not below.
3. Where there is more than one league within any given grade group, groupings shall be determined by team ability.
4. Grade divisions (Grade as of April 1st of current season).
   T-Ball—K, 1st and 2nd grades   Yearling—7th and 8th grades
   Colt B—3rd and 4th grades   Filly—9th thru 12 graders
   Colt A—5th and 6th grades

5. A player must play in three or more league games to be eligible for league playoffs.
6. If a team requests to be placed in a higher age bracket and in the opinion of the Sports Office staff could handle it, the request may be approved.

E. Waiver
1. All rosters are frozen immediately after the final practice game is played. A player may be added only by use of the waiver procedure at this time.
   a. Managers must obtain waiver forms from the Sports Office staff and must be filled out completely and signed by the League Director, before circulation for required number of manager's signatures,
   b. Waivers must be signed by managers in the same classification as the team adding the players.
   c. A wavered player may begin to play as soon as a Sports Office staff member accepts the completed form.
   d. New pitchers must be approved by the Sports Office and waivers must be signed by each manager of that league, except in the top division of each grade group where any rostered player (except non-residents) may pitch,
   e. No waivers will be accepted after the end of the first round of league play.
   f. **WARNING:** Any manager who is asked by another manager to sign a waiver is free to sign or not sign. The signature of a Sports Office staff member on the form does not constitute approval of the waiver.

G. Releases
   1. A player desiring a release must have a waiver form filled out, must secure the signature of the releasing manager, and must be authorized by the Sports Office before signing up with another team.
   2. A manager may drop a player from his roster only by writing a letter subject to approval by the Sports Office.

III. Team Eligibility

A. No team shall bear the name of, or any trade name of, any alcoholic or tobacco products. All team names including those incorporating a sponsor name are subject to approval of the League Director.

B. Rosters

1. A roster of players must be in the Sports Office by the specified date in the season. Rosters not turned in by this date will automatically release any player of her signature, and upon application to the Sports Office, a player may join any team that wants her.

2. The roster may not contain more than 18 players unless by special arrangement with the League Director. In 3/4 grade Colt B and 5/6 grade Colt A divisions all teams must carry a minimum of 13 players. In 7/8 grade Yearling and 9-12 grade Filly divisions all teams must carry a minimum of 12 players.

3. A roster must contain the name, address, city, zip code and phone number, signature, school, birth date and grade of each player and a parent signature.

4. In any case where a participant has deliberately falsified her record, those games in which she participated shall be forfeited and the player suspended.

5. All rostered players must live or attend school in Burbank at the start of the season. **Exception:** Each team will be allowed to have one non-resident player provided that the player's parent/guardian is an active coach or manager or participates actively in a team organizational role as approved by the Sports Office. This nonresident player must be noted as such on the roster. A player's residency will be established as of the first day of practice round for the league. Eligibility established at that date will stand for the remainder of the season. The nonresident player will be eligible to play any position <u>except pitcher</u> in these leagues.

6. Any player that puts her signature on two different rosters shall automatically be suspended until her case is brought before the Burbank Athletic Federation.

7. All rosters and waivers are subject to approval by the Burbank Athletic Federation with intentions of maintaining the leagues on an even competitive scale.

8. Managers must sign their rosters or waivers to certify that all ages and grades are correct.

9. Managers are responsible for the eligibility of all names of personnel on his roster.

10. All pitchers and CIF players must be identified on the roster.

11. All rosters are frozen immediately after the final practice game is played. A player may be added only by use of the waiver procedure at this time.

12. Each team may have one assistant manager and one assistant coach. Any changes must be cleared by the Sports Office.

13. Bat handlers must be listed on the team roster. Bat handlers are not eligible to play.

14. Only rostered members may sit on the bench with the team; no children, brothers, sisters, friends, etc. at anytime.

15. All prospective pitchers must participate in the practice round as a pitcher, and be seen pitching by a member of the Sports Office staff.

16. For the purpose of team classification, Sports Office staff may request to see a player pitch on the sideline if that player is a prospective pitcher.

17. All rosters and waivers are subject to approval by the B.A.F. with intentions of maintaining the leagues on an even competitive scale.

IV. Protests

A. Questions of fact cannot be protested. Protests that shall be received and considered are: Misrepresentation of a playing rule, wrongful application of a rule and a wrongly imposed penalty for a violation. Protests in the matter of judgment by the umpire are considered invalid.

B. When grounds for a protest arise in a game, only the manager or acting manager of the offended team must notify the plate umpire before the next pitch that the balance of the game is being played under protest. The plate umpire shall then immediately announce to the teams that the game is protested by one of the teams and is being played under protest.

C. The manager of the offended team at the time of his protest shall deposit a $5.00 protest fee with the umpire. In addition, the protest must be presented in writing, on an official protest blank, obtained from the park official or Sports Office and given to the League Director by the protesting manager within 24 hours of the scheduled time of the game under protest. An additional $5.00 must accompany the written protest.

D. The entire $10.00 deposit shall be returned if the protest is allowed. If the protest is not allowed, the entire $10.00 is forfeited to the Burbank Athletic Federation.

E. In case the game is continued under protest and the $5.00 fee paid to the umpire but the written protest and the additional $5.00 are not turned in to the Sports Office within 24 hours, there shall be no ruling. The protest shall be disallowed and the $5.00 forfeited to the Burbank Athletic Federation.

F. All protests shall be acted upon by the League Director as soon as possible after receiving the protest, and the decision shall be final.

G. At a playoff game, all protests shall be decided by the Sports Office supervisor in charge with game officials immediately.

V. Park Ground Rules

All ground rules will be explained by the umpires and/or park supervisor before game time. These will become the official ground rules for the game. Any situations not covered are left to the discretion of the umpire. It would be in the manager's best interest to ask pertinent questions during the pre-game meeting.

VI. Insurance/Players Medical Benefit Fund

All teams in the Hap Minor Leagues have included as a part of their league fees a membership in the Players' Medical Benefit Fund.

A. Claim procedure

1. Injured girl or team manager must obtain a claim form from the Sports Office.
2. A complete City Accident form must be filled out and filed.
3. Team manager must sign the form and return it to the Sports Office for forwarding to the claims office.
4. Players pay their own medical expenses and are reimbursed up to $500 per year.
5. Detailed instructions are available from the Sports Office.

VII. Selecting A Champion/Determining A Winner

A. Refer to the "Determining A Champion" letter sent to the managers at the beginning of league play.

VIII. Sportsmanship

A. Yelling at the opposing team will not be tolerated. No negative yelling will be allowed, including the harassment of the pitcher, officials or opposing players. One warning will be issued. After that, the game will be subject to forfeiture. Parents, coaches and managers are expected to serve as good examples.

B. No unison yelling will be allowed.

C. Good sportsmanship will be expected at all times, under all circumstances. This includes spectators and participants showing good sportsmanship.

D. Teams must participate in a courtesy hand-shake at the end of the game. Unsportsmanlike conduct will not be tolerated. Coaches and managers should also participate in post-game handshakes.

E. Encourage your own players.

Chapter 6

T-BALL Rules and Regulations

The rules of the National Federation of High School Associations shall be enforced in the Hap Minor/Ponytail Leagues unless amended below. Situations not specifically covered in these league rules shall be left to the discretion of the Local Athletic Federation Board of Directors and Sports Office staff.

I. Player's Eligibility

A. All players must be in good standing with the Burbank Athletic Federation.

B A player is not eligible until her signature and her parents signature appears on a team's roster. PENALTY for using a player not on a roster—FORFEITURE of all league games in which she played illegally, suspension of player and manager.

C. T-Ball teams are provided for boys and T-Ball teams are provided for girls. Therefore, girls shall not be permitted to play for a boys T-ball team nor shall boys be permitted to play for a girls T-Ball team.

D. Any player who participated in the Parochial League or any organized baseball or softball league in Burbank during the current season shall be eligible for the Ponytail T-Ball leagues. NOTE: No team may have more than 8 players who played Parochial League.

E. A player can play for only one baseball or one softball team under the jurisdiction of the Burbank Athletic Federation.

F. The following standards will be applied to the Ponytail League Classification procedure.

1. Team grouping is determined by the highest grade represented by any player on the team.
2. A player may play above her grouping but not below.
3. Where there is more than one league within a given grade group, groupings shall be determined by the grade level of the majority of the players on a specific team and/or by team ability. NOTE: Teams which have 50% or more players who played Parochial League can expect to be classified into higher divisions.
4. A player must play in three or more league games to be eligible for league playoffs.

G. Waiver

All rosters are frozen immediately after the final practice game is played. A player may be added only by use of the waiver procedure at the time.

    a. Forms may be obtained from the Sports Office and must be filled out completely and signed by the League Director before circulation for required number of managers signatures.

    b. As soon as the waiver is received and endorsed by the Sports Office, the player will be notified and immediately made eligible to play. Only members of the Sports Office staff may receive applications or waivers for transfers.

    c. Waivers must be signed by managers in the same classification as the team adding the player.

    d. The waiver procedure is valid only through the first half of the season. No waivers will be issued during the second half.

H. Release

1. A player desiring a release must have a waiver form filled out and the signature of the releasing manager secured and be authorized by the Sports Office before signing up with another team.
2. A manager may drop a player from his/her roster only by writing a letter which will be subject to the approval of the Sports Office.

II. Team Eligibility

A. No team shall bear the name or trade name of any alcoholic beverage. All team names are subject to approval of the Burbank Athletic Federation.

B. Rosters
1. A roster of Players must be in the Sports Office by the roster deadline. Rosters not turned in by this date will automatically release any player of her signature, and upon application to the Sports Office, the player may join any team that wants her.
2. The roster must have a minimum of 15 players and may not contain more than 18 players unless by special arrangement with the League Director.
3. A roster must contain the name, address, city, phone number, signature, school, birth date, and grade of each player.
4. In any case where a participant has deliberately falsified her record, those games in which she participated shall be forfeited and the player suspended.
5. All rostered players must live or attend school in Burbank at the start of the season. Exception: Each team will be allowed to have one non-resident player provided that the players parent/guardian is an active coach or manager or participates actively in a team organizational role as approved by the Sports Office. This non-resident player must be noted as such on the roster. A player's residency will be established as of the first day of practice round for the league. Eligibility established at that date will stand for the remainder of the season.
6. Any player that puts her signature on two different rosters shall automatically be suspended until she is brought before the Burbank Athletic Federation.
7. All rosters and waivers are subject to approval by the Burbank Athletic Federation with intentions of maintaining the leagues on an even but competitive scale.

8. Managers must sign their rosters or waivers to certify that all ages and grades are correct.

9. Managers are responsible for the eligibility of all names of personnel on his/her roster.

III. Manager's And Coach's Responsibility

A. All managers and coaches must be in good standing with the Burbank Athletic Federation.

B. Manager, coaches and "bat handler" signatures must appear on the official team roster or they will not be allowed to sit on the players' bench. "Bat handlers" are not eligible to play.

C. Managers are directly responsible to the Burbank Athletic Federation and the Park and Recreation Department for league fees, rosters, team business and conduct of players, coaches, parents, and spectators.

D. Managers are responsible for Players' Medical Benefit Fund forms and accident forms to be properly filled out and returned to the Sports Office.

E. Managers are responsible for keeping unauthorized persons out of his/her dugout and controlling the conduct of his/her team at all times.

F. It is the managers responsibility to prevent players from leaving the field and mingling with the spectators during the game.

G. Team managers will be responsible for keeping their teams off the general playing area until the conclusion of the preceding game.

H. Managers are responsible for the conduct of his team's spectators and will take all necessary steps to inform them of the rules, purpose and philosophy of the league.

I. Coaches will refrain from verbally coaching their players in a negative manner while they are on the field.

J. Managers must inform their players to report all accidents to the park supervisor at the time they occur so that a Park and Recreation Accident Form may be completed.

K. Managers and coaches may not smoke in the dugout or on the playing field.

L. All coaches shall be required to comply with the requirements established by the Park and Recreation Department for background checks for volunteers.

IV. Insurance/Players Medical Benefit Fund

All teams in the Ponytail Leagues have included as a part of their league fees a membership in the Players' Medical Benefit Fund.

Claim Procedure

1. Injured player or team manager must obtain a claim form from the Sports Office.
2. A complete City Accident form must be filled out and filed.
3. Team manager must sign the form and return it to the Sports Office for forwarding to the claims office.
4. Players pay their own medical expenses and are reimbursed up to $ 500 per year.
5. Detailed instructions are available from the Sports Office.

V. Sportsmanship

A. Good sportsmanship is expected at all times under all circumstances. Teams must participate in courtesy handshake at the end of the game. Unsportsmanlike conduct will not be tolerated.

B. No derogatory yelling at the other team is permitted. The game will be forfeited if such behavior is noted.

C. No unison yelling.

D. No negative yelling at the opposing team or officials. This does not teach boys and girls good sportsmanship and will not be condoned.

E. Parents, coaches and managers shall set the example for the players.

VI. Equipment

A. Game ball is official leather 10" softball for girls' T-Ball and deBeer TuffLite (BI19S) for boys' T-Ball. List of acceptable brand names is available from the Sports Office.

    1. Home team will furnish one new ball for the game.

    2. Visiting team will furnish one new ball for the game.

    3. If both balls are lost during the course of the game, the home team shall furnish the third suitable ball and the visiting team the fourth, etc.

    4. Home team shall have first choice of balls at the end of the game.

B. Bats must be in conformance with the following:

    1. Either an official hardball or softball bat in accordance with National Federation specifications is acceptable.

    2. Metal bats must be continuous one piece. Rubber knobbed bats are unacceptable.

C. All bats must be equipped with a safety grip 10 inches to 18 inches in length.

D. All pitchers, batters and runners must wear complete safety helmets. The wrap-around headgear is unacceptable.

E. Participants must wear close-toed shoes while playing. The multi-purpose rubber-cleated shoe is acceptable. Steel cleats are prohibited. Managers and coaches must also wear appropriate shoes. This type of shoe is also used in Soccer and Flag Football.

F. Catchers must wear complete protective equipment including chest protector, mask with throat guard, shin guards and use a proper glove. The complete safety helmet shall be required.

G. All players must have a glove.

VII. Ground Rules

The umpire shall establish ground rules before game time. These will become the official rules for this game. Any situation not covered shall be left to the discretion of the umpire. It would be in the manager's best interest to ask pertinent questions in the pre-game meeting.

VIII. Game Rules

A. At the start of the game, each team shall designate either their coach or manager as team representative. This individual shall meet with the umpire(s) prior to game time to discuss ground rules, official starting time, etc. and shall thereafter be the only individual to enter the playing field for the purpose of necessary time-outs, rules interpretations by the game officiates) or player assistance (i.e.: injury, equipment repair, etc.). Abuse of this privilege by either coaches or managers may result in the suspension of the offending individuals.

B. Pitcher will field her position at 46 feet with one foot touching the rubber (permanent mound).

C. Bases will be set at 60 feet.

D. The game shall be one hour long, starting when the first batter enters the batter's box. The umpire's watch is the official time. Umpires will announce the last batter; incomplete innings will not be completed. No game will last longer than 7 innings or one hour, whichever occurs first.

E. Game time is forfeit time. Ten players will play in the game at one time with the tenth player playing as rover. A team may start with seven players, but may not continue with less than seven.

F. All players in attendance must be placed on the line-up and must bat in proper rotation. No change is permitted in the official batting order. If a player appears late, her name should be placed at the bottom of the batting order.

G. Every player must play in every game. Free substitution will be used during the games. Players may be removed and then inserted into defensive positions at will. Pinch runners may be used for sick and injured players only. Pinch runners can only be the player who made the last out.

H. Two coaches from the defensive team may be on the field to help direct play. Coaches may not interfere or participate in any play.

I. Baserunning

1. Once the pitcher or catcher has control of the ball inside her circle, the ball becomes dead and play is stopped. Runners less than half way to the next base must return to the original base. Runners more than half way to the next base will be entitled to that base.

2. No stealing of bases is allowed. A runner may not leave the base until the ball is hit or the runner will be called out. If a runner leaves too soon, the hit will not count, the batter will bat again, and the other runners will return to the bases originally occupied.

3. If a ball stays in the designated live areas on a overthrow, all runners may advance at their own risk.

J. Batting

1. The tee will be placed in front of home plate, not on it, with point of the tee facing the pitcher.

2. Players must use a full swing in each attempt when hitting off the tee. No bunting.

3. A ball swung at and missed is a strike. The batter will be declared out with any combination of three (3) strikes.

4. If the batter strikes the tee and any portion of the ball and the ball goes fair, it is playable.

5. If the batter strikes only the tee and no portion of the ball, a strike will be called and the ball is dead, whether it goes fair or not. Whether the batter makes contact with the ball and/or the tee is the sole judgment of the umpire.

6. A foul ball will be called on a batted ball which:

   a. remains in the arc area.

   b. lands outside the fair area.

    c. lands fair and then rolls foul or back into the arc without being touched.

    * The first two foul balls will be counted as strikes, but it will be considered a foul ball only on additional hits. Runners may not advance on foul balls.

7. The arc area shall be an 8-foot radius circle around home plate. If a player hits a fair or foul ball and her bat is thrown out of the arc area, she shall be called out and the baserunners must return to their original bases. If in the umpire's opinion, the bat is dropped in the circle and rolls out of the circle, the batter/runner is not out.

8. During each half of an inning, the batting team will bat until three outs are made or until ten batters have completed their turns at bat. The umpire should announce that the tenth batter is coming up. After completing her at-bat, that half of the inning will be considered completed.

9. Catcher must be outside the circle, behind the plate, with the ball on the tee, before the batter hits. PENALTY: Batter is out.

K. The infield fly rule is not in effect.

L. There are no protests in T-Ball.

M. Players should run on and off the field.

N. Circle around pitchers mound will be 8-foot radius.

O. No scores or standings will be kept.

PARTICIPATION AWARDS Each player will receive a participation award at the conclusion of the season.

Chapter 7

Coaching T-Ball Players

T-Ball is for girls in Kindergarten, first and second grades, usually 6 and 7 years old to participate in softball. The bases are 60 feet and pitcher is in contact with the plate at 46 feet. T-Ball is designed to give the children a recreational learning experience in sports. No scores are kept and should not be referred to as part of the game. The four physical basics of this game are throwing, catching, batting and running.

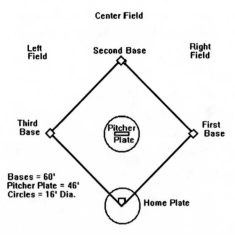

As the coach, you will be required to demonstrate all of the skills that a player must acquire in order to play this game. Make sure you can get their attention whenever you show them how to do what it is you want them to do. Make it fun and use your sense of humor. Each skill has its very own way of being performed, and that is your job to teach.

Please remember that youngsters in this category have a fear of being hit by the ball. They want to play and not get hurt or to hurt anyone else. The glove is more of a hindrance than a help in the beginning, and they have no confidence in it. So, understanding where the fear is with the children, it should help you devise your practice program.

A problem that you will encounter is with the bat and batting practice. Some youngsters forget the hazards associated with swinging the bat freely. And when one is near and they get their hands on it, they start swinging without looking to see who is around them. I feel this requires constant supervision.

In T-Ball it is the Pitcher who is most apt to be injured by a batted ball and the Catcher by a thrown bat. Always have the catcher stand outside the circle, behind the batter, and on the opposite side she is swinging from. For instance, the batter is right handed and in the left side batting box, the catcher will stand on the opposite side, furthermost away from where the bat will fall.

Start their training session in the same way the older girls do, with a throw and catch warm-up. Instruct them in "how to" do both at the same time. Each child wants to be a good player and your encouragement will help them become that.

Their very next step is to understand where they play on the playing field. Where the bases are and the pitchers mound. What the catcher does and where she plays. Let them understand where the infield is and the outfield is. Children this age are very smart, and will pick up anything that you say as gospel. Now is the time to begin using the language of the game, referring for instance to the "dugout" and how they use it during a game.

Player positions on the field.

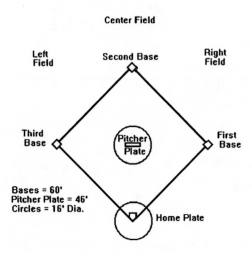

During your first practice gathering, you must take all of the players, start-ing at home plate and walk them around the bases, explaining which base they are on at the time. Then with everyone at home plate, have each player run the bases and call out which base she is tagging. After all of the players have called bases, gather them at second base and explain where the infield is.

With the team at second base, have them face the outfield and explain where it is. With youngsters in tow, lead them to left field and explain the position, repeat it for center field and right field. Returning to home plate, show them the foul lines that extend to the outfield. Now everyone has an idea about the playing field. Show where the pitching mound is and where the catcher plays.

Assign positions and ask the girls to take their places on the field as you make the assignments. Make it a game to see if they know where to go. In T-ball, you have ten players on the field. The tenth player is called a Rover. The

Rover is normally played midway between first and second base. If you have more than enough girls, have them take infield positions as alternates.

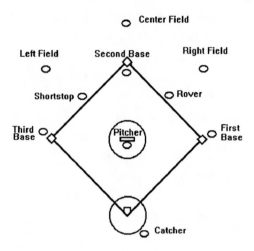

Throwing the Ball.

The hands of children are small and the ball seems to them larger than what they have experienced before. Have them grasp the ball with all fingers, the most important part being with the thumb directly opposite the middle finger and under the ball. This is the basic grip for them to use.

The middle finger is the strongest finger of the hand and adds snap to the throw. Kinesthetically speaking, the thumb will release first and the ball will be propelled by the first, middle and third fingers. It is the forward snap of the wrist which whips these fingers forward adding velocity to the ball.

The throwing of the ball without instruction will be somewhere between an overhand throw and sidearm. All children have their own way of throwing a ball, which simply comes naturally to them. What we want to do, is teach the overhand throwing method. If done properly, their accuracy will improve almost immediately, perhaps not in the vertical plane, but definitely in the horizontal.

Overhand is when the throwing arm is horizontal to the ground, the elbow bent in such a way as to place the ball almost behind the head above the shoulder. The thrower turns sideways with the gloved hand towards the receiver, steps forward on that foot, twists her body as she throws and ends up facing the receiver.

If the foot she steps forward on is pointing directly towards the receiver, the balls flight should be directly at the receiver. In teaching the player how to throw, we throw "to" someplace, not "at" some place. Always emphasize "to". There are four movements involved with the throw. Arm raised and cocked with player balanced. Step towards target, rotation of hips, rotation of trunk and arm extension with a wrist snap.

Catching the Ball.

This is the hardest to teach to the youngest players. First, they are afraid of being hit by the ball and secondly they have no glove skills. It isn't unusual for a girl to flinch while trying to make a catch. Players must understand that this game is played through the eyes and they must watch the ball at all times. No closing the eyes or looking away from the ball.

Balls tossed below the waist can be caught with the pocket facing up and the free hand is used to trap the ball from falling out. From head to chest level, the pocket faces forward, thumb in, then moved to accept the ball in the pocket trapped by the free hand. The player uses it like a shield, protecting herself and grabbing the ball. Overhead balls are treated the same way with the pocket turned to face the incoming ball and trapped by the free hand.

T-Ball Batting.

The very first thing we do is show the proper way to grip the bat and how it is swung. Indicate at what level you want the bat held in the ready position and show them how the wrists rotate as the bat is swung through it's arc. Show her how to move her body forward, shifting her weight from the back foot to the front foot as she contacts a ball. Have all the players, without bats, hit an imaginary ball using their body motions.

What we want to accomplish here is an understanding of how to use all of the body in hitting the ball. Most children will begin batting by using arm power only to swing the bat. Therefore, when the batter cocks up to swing, she must rotate her hips and shoulders. As her swing begins from the stance you have place her in, show her how to rotate for maximum impact.

Let's go over the steps quickly. The girl in the batters box raises the bat, places her balance on the back foot, rotates her hip and shoulders away from the Tee. On the swing, as she shifts her weight to the front foot, twists hips, shoulders and swings the bat with arms extended in an arc towards the ball. Allow the swing to follow through to her other side, then drop the bat inside the batting circle.

Set up a Tee with the batter's box outlined on the ground to show the player where to stand. Without using a bat, have each player go through the hitting motion swinging an imaginary bat. Next have each player using a bat, take turns at hitting five balls off the Tee. Indicate to the player where she must stand to put the ball down the third base line, the first base line, and to center field.

T-Ball Base Running.

We begin by explaining to the team that the baserunner cannot leave the base until the ball has been hit from the Tee. Each runner must be in contact at the "ready" on any base. She may stand directly on the base with her toes hooked on the edge like a starting block, or in the lead-off position with her trailing foot in contact ready to sprint.

Two conditions will quickly return her to her starting base. If the ball is a fly and caught by a fielder, she must return a quickly as possible to the safety of the base or be caught off base and called out. Second is if the ball has been thrown to the pitcher and she has not made it halfway to the safety of her next base.

T-Ball Throwing & Catching Drills.

Divide your team into two equal number of players. Place half of the team along the foul line extending just beyond first base to the outfield. Place the other half of your team on the field facing the foul line and the other players. Get at least eight feet between each player and a throwing distance of approximately 12 feet.

Each girl on the foul line is given a ball. Each girl playing must have a glove. Now, under your supervision, have them begin their throwing and catching exercise. Give plenty of attention to their throwing style, and encourage the catching effort. As the players improve, open the distance between them.

At every practice, as the girls arrive, they should pair up and start their warm up with the throwing and catching drill. This immediately brings their focus on softball. Improvements will come in leaps and bounds at each new practice or game. This is also the pre-game warm up to get them into the spirit of things.

Catching the Infield Ground Ball

During practice and game play, the player on the field is always in the flexed or bent knee position, facing home plate, body in balance with her glove at the "ready". As the ball comes to her, she must move laterally either to her left or right to get in front of the ball. Next the glove must go down until it touches the ground, pocket facing the ball and her free hand above the glove ready to trap the ball.

The free hand does two things. It traps the ball and instantly prepares the ball to be taken and thrown, secondly it keeps the ball from bouncing out of the glove and into the players face. At times there will be a bounce, but the player can raise the glove quickly by either lifting the glove with her arm or lifting her upper body.

Catching the Infield Fly Ball

The player comes up from the flexed knee stance and must move in either of four directions; forward, backward, to the left or to the right to be in front of the ball. The glove goes up and over her head and face, pocket facing the ball. The free hand is also raised to trap the ball and give quick access for a throw. She must watch the ball all of the way into her glove.

T-Ball Infield Drills.

Position all of your players in the "ready" stance, slightly down with knees flexed, glove open and back straight. Instruct the infield how to move laterally and get in front of the ball to catch it.

With players & alternates at first, rover, second, shortstop, and third base. Position yourself midway between the pitchers plate and home base. Using a bat, softly hit the ball to any player and have that player trap and return the ball to you. Encourage the player to throw the ball overhand.

If you have hit the ball to the third baseman and she has returned the ball to you, have her alternate move into position for the next ball hit to that base. Alternate all players so that all players get a chance to trap the ground ball. It is important that every player have a chance to participate in these drills.

Eventually, as the players improve, you will stand at home plate and use a bat to softly hit the ball to a receiver. The receiver must make an attempt to throw the ball home. What we are looking for at this point, is who can throw the ball the furthest. Why? We are looking for our third baseman and alternate.

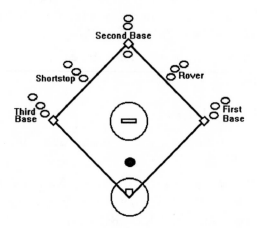

Once we get the ground balls down, we work on hitting short fly balls to the infielders. "Pop flies" you might call it. From home plate begin your infield drills with grounders all around, then insert the fly balls and encourage quick "get" and quick "throw home."

Catching the Outfield Ground Ball.

This is the same as catching an infield grounder, but a little different in as much as it may be a bouncing ground ball. The outfielder must charge the ball, moving laterally left or right to be in the proper position to knock the ball down. If it's a roller, she scoops it up with the glove pocket facing the ball and her free hand trapping it.

If she takes it on the bounce, she catches the ball at mid body level with the pocket facing forward and the thumb pointing down. Again the free hand is used to trap, recover and throw.

Catching the Outfield Fly Ball.

The player comes up from the flexed knee stance and must move in either of four directions; forward, backward, to the left or to the right to be in front of the ball. The glove goes up and over her head and face, pocket facing the ball. The free hand is also raised to trap the ball and give quick access for a throw. She must watch the ball all of the way into her glove. Same as the infield fly ball, however when the ball is hit long, it is harder to assess where it will land.

Judging a long balls flight is difficult, especially when it is coming directly towards the player. When you have a visual angle of the balls arc, it makes it easier to judge. Most errors made here are from not going back soon enough.

T-Ball Outfield Drills

With a player at first, second, third base and the pitcher in the pitchers circle. Break the remaining team into three equal groups if possible. Have one group form a line at the left field position facing home in line which places them in sequence to play the fielders position. Do the same for center field and right field.

Position yourself near the pitchers circle. Bat a ground ball to left field, have the player trap the ball and return it to third base. Third base will catch the ball and throw it to the pitcher, who in turn gives it back to you. Repeat the same to center field and have the fielder trap the ball and throw to second base. Second base will catch the ball and throw it to the pitcher, who in turn gives it back to you. You repeat the same exercise with right field who returns to first base, the pitcher and back to you. Encourage the players to throw the ball overhand.

Alternate all players so that all players get a chance to catch the ground ball. It is important that every player have a chance to participate in these drills. Shift the fielding lines so that each line plays in all three outfield positions.

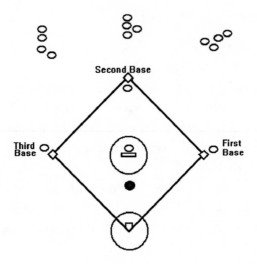

Position yourself near the home plate. Bat a fly ball to left field, have the player catch the ball and return it to third base. Third base will catch the ball and throw it to the pitcher, who in turn gives it back to you. Repeat the same to center field and have the fielder catch the ball and throw to second base. Second base will catch the ball and throw it to the pitcher, who in turn gives it back to you. You repeat the same exercise with right field who returns to first base, the pitcher and back to you.

Alternate all players so that all players get a chance to catch the fly ball. It is important that every player have a chance to participate in these drills. Shift the fielding lines so that each line plays in all three outfield positions.

How to play Defense.

Playing defense is teaching the team where the play is to be made. It may be to any base which will result in a runner being called out. It may be a combination of bases and outs. This is really the fun part of coaching, where you give them information that is as important as their playing skills. Their self esteem grows as their knowledge of the game grows.

Get the lead runner: The goal here is to get the player in scoring position out. It can be a forced out for a runner going from second base to third base, or from first base to second base.

Infielder backup: Infielders backup throws to any base. An example could be the Rover throwing to second, and the shortstop backs up the second baseman. Outfielders also backup the infielders who are working with each other. This means that every player not involved in a play should be backing up the throw.

Outfielder to relay: Is important to prevent a runner from advancing to another base. The outfielder must gather the ball and release it quickly to the relay player. The relay may be any infielder who moves out to shorten the distance from a long hit ball. More often than not, the relay player is the shortstop.

Outfielder backup: All outfielders back each other up in the event a ball gets away from the outfielder in the best position to make the play. Center field may call for any ball hit to the outfield.

A player may not throw as well, or bat, or run as well as another player, but when she knows where the play is, that makes her important. She feels good about herself, because she knows! And when the ball comes to her, she is confident as to what she must do. Knowledge is power. She is given the chance to make choices in the game.

In T-Ball, we try to keep it as basic and simple as possible for the player to grasp the game. One simple plan is, if in doubt, get the ball to the pitcher. No player may advance if the pitcher has the ball, nor may she continue to advance if the pitcher has the ball before the runner has reached the half way point between bases. Simple first rule.

Next simple rule is if no one is on base and the batter hits the ball and it is fielded, the throw should be to first base for an out. Now this is where you need a good arm on third base. What the batter will want to do is hit down the third baseline which gives her the greatest chance to reach first base. Why? Because the throw from third to first is the longest between bases. If the ball is fielded by an outfielder, the play is to second base unless fielded by right field.

Next rule will be when a runner is on first base and the batted ball is fielded by the third baseman, shortstop or second baseman to play the ball to second base. It's good for an out and holds the runner at first base. Now if your team is in their second year of T-Ball, you may elect to coach the second baseman into throwing to first for a double play.

In the event the ball is fielded by the Rover or the first baseman, you tag first and throw to the pitcher. I don't encourage throwing to second base for a double play for one reason. The runner is vulnerable to being hit in the back by a thrown ball. I want no tears or fears. If the ball is fielded by an outfielder, the play is to second base regardless.

Next rule will be with runners on first and second base and the batted ball is fielded by the third baseman, shortstop or second baseman to play the ball to third base. It's good for an out and holds the runners at first and second base. Now if your team is in their second year of T-Ball, you may elect to coach the third baseman into throwing to second base for a double play.

In the event the ball is fielded by the Rover or the first baseman, you tag first base and throw to the pitcher or third base. No throws to the second baseman. If the ball is fielded by an outfielder, the play is to second base regardless.

When the bases are "loaded", or a runner is on all bases, then the fielder tags the base closest to her and throws to the catcher at home plate. You already know all of the options for making multiple outs in this situation, but for girls in this league it becomes to complex. If the ball is fielded by an outfielder, depending on which outfielder and where, the throw is to the base nearest to the outfielder.

So far so good for making choices of fielded balls and where they can or should be played depending on baserunners. This is a lot of stuff for youngsters to learn and be confident with, but it happens that way. And any mistakes made by their choices or lack of physical abilities is also okay. Everything is always okay, okay?

Fly-outs are another story. Every player on the field has the potential to catch a fly ball for an out. What we want to stress here to all of the players, is to keep their "heads" in the game. When a batter steps to the Tee and addresses the ball, the field must look to see where the runners are, or if there are runners on bases.

If there are no runners on any of the bases and a fly ball is caught, it is a routine out with the batter returning to the dugout. In T-Ball, no runner can lead off from the base before the ball is hit by the batter. Usually what happens with a runner, she will start the moment the ball is hit and head for the safety of the next base before the ball is caught.

If the runner has remained on base until after the ball is caught, she can then run for the next base without jeopardy of having to beat the ball back to the base she just left. If the runner has left prior to the catch, she may be put out with a throw to that base by the fielder if the ball reaches the base before the runner returns.

This is the situation we want the girls to understand and be aware of who has left a base so they can try for the second out or a double play. It happens in T-Ball. It's the easiest way for youngsters to make a double play. Let's have an example here. If the bases were "loaded" and the shortstop caught the ball, she should immediately throw to third for an expected out. Not to second where she may hit a girl moving in her direction.

Following this further, if the second baseman caught the ball and her runner is off base, she can tag second, step inside and try for a throw to third to catch the runner who left third base. Now if the third baseman caught the ball, she tags third base, avoids throwing to second and checks first base for a possibility.

The player with the greatest number of choices in the infield is the pitcher. If she catches a fly ball, all bases are open for her to make her choice from. Her first choice should be third base to pick off a player who is considered in a scoring position. Surprisingly, the pitcher does make a lot of outs on pop flies and dribbling grounders.

The infield players have the greater opportunity for the double or the triple play than the outfielders have. An outfielder who has caught a fly ball should throw in to the base nearest to her, the other option being to throw in to the pitcher.

Defensive Drills.
Throwing the bases:

Our simplest drill will be breaking the team into four equal groups that we can assign to first base, second base, third base and home plate. The distance between each base is the same, making the drill an even challenge for each player.

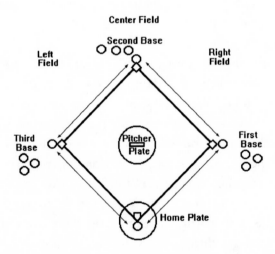

Starting from home plate the ball is thrown to third, from third to second, from second to first and then to home. The player at home throws to first, first throws to second, second throws to third, and third throws to home.

That is one circuit. Have each of the girls who participated go to the rear of her line and wait for her next time to participate. To add some fun to the throwing and catching game we begin timing how long it takes to complete the circuit. After each circuit, call out the time taken and encourage the girls to try to beat the best time recorded.

We accomplish two things here. First we get their competitiveness going and secondly we get them to focus on throwing and catching the ball. Just a little competition nulls the fear of the ball and makes each one want to do her best. For beginners, this is a lot of fun.

Infield Position Drill.

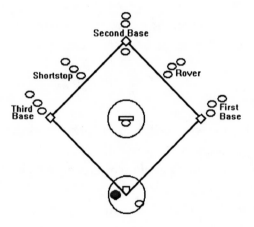

Assign players and alternates to each position in the infield. That will be first base, Rover, second base, shortstop, third base, pitcher and catcher positions. You will take up your position at home plate to hit the ball either on the ground to the infielder, or a soft fly ball. The fly ball will depend on how well your team has progressed.

Here's how it goes. When you hit the ball to the fielder, you call out the base where the play is to be made. If it is to the shortstop, call out for first base. The shortstop fields the ball and throws to first. First in turn now throws to the pitcher who in turn throws to the catcher, who will return it to you.

After each infielder and alternate, including the pitcher has thrown to first, make the play to second base. The second baseman follows the example set by the first baseman by returning the ball to the pitcher who in turn throws to the catcher, who will return the ball to you.

After each infielder and alternate, including the pitcher has thrown to second, make the play to third base. The third baseman follows the example set by the second baseman by returning the ball to the pitcher who in turn throws to the catcher, who will return the ball to you.

That's the drill! If you run the drill often, I would suggest that you shift players around so that each player gets a chance to play at every position. In that sense, everyone knows the difficulty of playing at any of the infield positions. And you get a better understanding of the teams weaknesses and strengths.

Infield Doubles Drill.

This drill is a little more complex than the previous drill and may be only for your players who are in the second year of T-Ball. However, it all depends on your players individual involvement and abilities.

Assign players and alternates to each position in the infield. That will be first base, Rover, second base, shortstop, third base, pitcher and catcher positions. You will take up your position at home plate to hit the ball either on the ground to the fielder, or a soft fly ball. The fly ball will depend on how well your team has progressed.

Here's how it goes. Tell the team there is a runner on first base, then you hit the ball to the infielder, you call out the base where the play is to be made. If it is to the shortstop, call out for second base. The shortstop fields the ball and throws to the second baseman who tags the base then throws to first base. First in turn now throws to the pitcher who in turn throws to the catcher, who will return it to you.

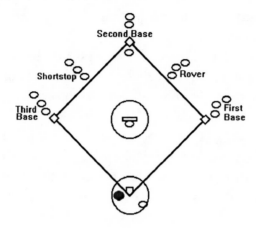

You may also expand this idea for runners on first and second, and have the shortstop or your selected infielder make the play to third or to tag the base and throw to the next base to occupied. I would suggest that you shift players around so that each player gets a chance to play at every position.

How to Play Offense.

Offense in T-Ball boils down to batting, running, observing and taking base coach's instructions. Hitting towards third base is the most basic of these simple offensive moves. It gives the runner more time to reach first base safely and it is the farthest throw an infielder can make to another base, the exception being second base to home.

You must teach the players how to take advantage of defense when situations arise such as a wild throw to the pitcher, catcher or throw to a base. The player should be ready to take the next base without having to be told by you that an opportunity has arrived.

The player must take the proper stance in the batting box and measure the ball height with her bat extended to the Tee. When given the signal that she can swing, it should be with all she's got. With good contact, she drops the bat inside the circle and goes for it. If it rolls foul of course she's called back to try again.

Each player should understand that when she is a baserunner on a base, that she must run to the next base when the ball is hit fair. She may continue to run as long as she thinks she can reach the next base safely or is encouraged by the base coach.

She must be aware of two simple rules. If the ball is a fly-out she must return as quickly a possible to safety of the base she just left to avoid being put out. If not a fly-out and she is on first base, she must be on the run after contact is made.

T-Ball Batting Practice.

Using "knerf" or "woofle" balls is highly recommended in the drill for several reasons. The thin plastic skinned ball filled with holes does not have the ability to injure anyone the way a regulation ball could. It comes in all sizes, and in the same size as the recommended league ball listed under T-Ball equipment.

Using the knerf ball removes the fear of being hit by the girls playing as fielders. You accomplish several things in this practice. Players learn to use the glove for ground and fly balls. Batters learn proper batting habits and you get a chance to evaluate the players abilities. Build their confidence with encouragement.

If you have more than one Tee, divide your players into groups based on the number of Tee's you have. Three Tee's, then you'll have three groups of equal number. Assuming you have a diamond, go to the area just beyond first base, and set your Tee's in the foul area so the ball can be batted into the fair ball area or outfield.

T-Ball Batting Practice

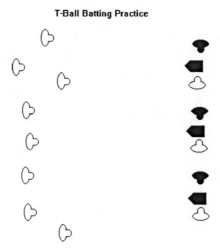

Set your Tee's twenty feet apart and assign one girl to bat at each Tee you have. Fan out the other members of the group, facing the Tee at twenty to twenty five feet distance. A coach or assistant will work with the girls who are batting. She will Tee-up the ball and instruct the player in proper stance and batting motions.

The remainder of the group, facing the Tee's will field the balls as they are hit and throw them back to the coach at that Tee. The Tee coach is in position to encourage and instruct both the batter and the fielder. Everyone is involved in the practice. Each girl will take ten turns at bat, then exchange positions with the next batter from the field.

T-Ball Running Drill

Setting up to sprint from the base is the baserunners next most important thing to learn. Some runners stand over the base facing the one they will run to with their kick-off foot against the base edge for a starting block kick. The runner must watch the batter to make contact, then jump start on the run.

Starting at home plate, line the team up for their sprint runs to the first base. On "GO", have a girl run to first, cross it and turn to her right, returning to the base. Bring up the next runner to home plate. Have the runner on first base ready to sprint to second base. On "GO" the runner on first sprints to second and the girl at home, repeats the first runners sprint to first base. All players in sequence, will run all bases until all players have completed the drill.

This can be given some variances to add fun. Assume the girl gets a double, have her rounding first and run to second, and time her effort. You can do the same for a triple. Only you will know, so keep the times close enough so that no runner is embarrassed and build some competitive spirit.

Competition Running Drill:

This is a fun drill where two players race each other around the bases in opposite directions. Make the match-up as even as possible, then on your signal one player heads for third base and the other goes for first base. The player who headed for first base passes just inside of second base and the other player goes just outside of second base. The one to cross home plate first is the winner.

A variation on this drill is to turn it into a relay race with a softball being the baton and passed to the next runner at home plate. It is an aerobic exercise which forces the girls to develop and give a best effort in practice. Everyone is involved and having fun while gaining a level of confidence in their sprinting.

The Game Practice.

This is the old time game of "work up" baseball, once played on sand lots all over the country. It was a lot of fun for the players because you had a chance to play every position in the game.

Assign a player to every position on the field. Those not assigned will become the batting bench. The rules are quite simple. If the batter hits the ball and safely makes it to first base, well and good. However if she is put out in the process of the fielded ball reaching first before she does, she goes to the left field position and the catcher joins the batting bench.

Everyone advances one position. Left field goes to center, center to right field, right field to third base, third base goes to shortstop, shortstop goes to second, second base goes to Rover, Rover goes to first, first base goes to pitcher, and pitcher becomes the catcher. That holds for any forced out.

A fly-out is a different story. A fly ball is hit into the infield and is caught by the shortstop. The shortstop advances to the batting bench, and the batter retires to left field. Every position behind shortstop now moves up one position. Third going to shortstop, etc.. In the event of a forced out double, everyone moves forward two positions.

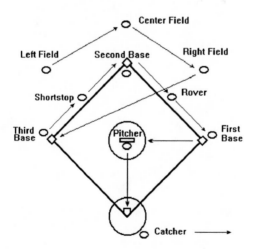

In the event we have a fly-out and a forced out double. The player who caught the fly goes to the batting bench. Everyone who had a position behind the fielder who caught the fly ball, moves ahead two positions, everyone ahead of the fielder moves forward, one. The batter who hit the fly-out ends up at center field, and the forced out goes to left field.

Triples are handled in the same way to advance players towards the batting bench. Now the batting bench has it's own constraints. A player who has successfully completed three runs is retired to left field advancing all other players. This evens the playing field and continues to move the game forward.

Kids love this game, and I guess that's where the old saw comes from "out in left field." Man, he's out in left field! You'll like it also since you get a chance to do some fun coaching and become the plate umpire.

Chapter 8

Rules For Colt-B

Third and Fourth Grade
(Exceptions From Ponytail Rules)
The rules of the National Federation of High School Associations shall be enforced in the Hap Minor/Ponytail Leagues unless amended below. Situations not specifically covered in these league rules shall be left to the discretion of the Local Athletic Federation Board of Directors and Sports Office staff.

The Beginning Ponytail Softball program is designed to be an introductory experience for young softball players. The emphasis should be on fun and learning and the competitive aspect should be kept very low key. Managers and coaches should explain the purpose of this program to their spectators in order for the girls to have the best experience possible.

Game Length

Game length will be 7 innings or no new inning after one hour and fifteen minutes, whichever comes first. Once an inning has started it must be completed. **Exception:** Radical Run rule (A radical score game with a ten run lead will be continued only at the request of the losing team after one hour of game time has expired. At a 15 run lead, the game will be continued only at the request of the winning and losing teams. However, the game will end when time limit has expired.

Batting

A. After ball four, tee will be brought in for the batter. **Exception:** (Top Colt-B Division will be granted the walk to first. No Tee will be used.) Batter will retain strike count and will be declared out with any combination of three strikes. The following rules will apply when hitting off the tee:

1. Tee will be placed in front of home plate, not on it, with the point of the tee facing the pitcher.
2. Player must use a full swing in each attempt when hitting off the tee. No bunting: The batter must be in the batter's box and use standard stance and step. She must take a full swing. If she does not, she will receive one warning, and on the second offense, be called out. Runners will return to their bases.
3. A ball swung at and missed is a strike.
4. If the batter strikes the tee and any portion of the ball and the ball goes fair, it is playable.
5. If the batter strikes the tee and no portion of the ball, a strike will be called and the ball is dead, whether it goes fair or not. Whether the batter makes contact with the ball and/or the tee is the sole judgment of the umpire.
6. A foul ball will be called on a batted ball which:
   a. remains in the are area.
   b. lands outside the fair area.
   c. lands fair and then rolls foul or back into the arc without being touched. The first two foul balls will be counted as strikes, but it will be considered a foul ball only on additional hits. Runners may not advance on foul balls.
7. The arc shall be 8' radius circle around home plate. If a player hits a fair or foul ball and her bat is thrown out of the arc area, she shall be called out and the baserunners must return to their original bases. If

in the umpire's opinion, the bat is dropped in the circle and rolls out of the circle, the batter/runner is not out.

8. During each half of an inning, the batting team will bat until three outs are made or until ten batters have completed their turns at bat. The umpire should announce that the tenth batter is coming up. After completing her at-bat, the half of the inning will be considered completed.

9. Catcher must be outside the circle, behind the plate, with the ball on the tee, before the batter hits. **Penalty:** Batter is out.

Pitching

A. Pitching Distance: 32 feet. When tee is brought in, the pitcher must stand at 46 foot permanent mount with at least one foot on the rubber.

Baserunning

A. During the pitching, the baserunners must abide by regulation baserunning rules. When the ball is on the "tee", the baserunners must remain on the base until the ball is legally hit. A runner may score:

1. On a fair hit ball,
2. On a foul ball that is legally caught,
3. On catcher's interference, hit by pitch, or base on balls (top division) if forced.

B. Runners may not steal or advance on Ball Four. Dead ball. **Exception:** (Top Colt-B Division)

C. Stealing home from third base shall not be permitted. A runner who is off third base illegally and has passed home plate shall be declared out by the umpire. A runner drawing a throw at home plate while attempting to acquire the right to that base illegally is considered off third base at her own risk and may be touched out before she returns safely to third base. If she touches home plate, the umpire shall declare her out.

D. A runner may not score on a passed ball or a wild pitch. **Note:** A ball rebounding off the backstop and fielded by another player shall be treated the same as if the catcher had thrown the ball to the pitcher.

E. Batter is out on dropped third strike.

F. A baserunner cannot score or steal a base on a return throw or battery error from the catcher to the pitcher. A baserunner may steal second or third base when the ball leaves the pitcher's hand and before the ball leaves the catcher's hand on the return throw to the pitcher. Baserunning rules pertaining to a runner on third base remain in effect.

Base Coaches

A. A coach or a coach with a player may coach the bases.

Team Batting

A. Teams must field a minimum of 7 players or forfeit. Teams will bat straight through their lineup. Free substitution of all players is allowed.

B. During each half of an inning, the batting team will bat until three outs are made or until ten batters have completed their turns at bat. The umpire should announce that the tenth batter is coming up. After she completes her at-bat, that half of the inning will be considered completed.

Safety

Managers should instruct their catchers to stand clear when the "tee" is being used. All players should be instructed as to the proper way of dropping their bat as opposed to throwing their bat after they hit the ball.

Equipment

A. Official softball bats may be used. Official Little League bats may be used but must have handles taped. All bats must be equipped with a safety grip 10 inches to 18 inches in length.

B. Balls are official leather 11" softball optic yellow RIF core .47, non-glazed.

1. Home team will furnish one new ball for the game.
2. Visiting team will furnish one new ball for the game.
3. If both balls are lost during the course of the game, the home team shall furnish the third suitable ball and the visiting team the fourth, etc.
4. Home team shall have first choice of balls at the end of the game.

C. All batters and runners must wear complete safety helmets. The wrap-around headgear is unacceptable.

D. Participants must wear close-toed shoes while playing. The multi-purpose rubber-cleated shoe is acceptable. Steel cleats are prohibited. Managers and coaches must also wear appropriate shoes.

E. Catchers must wear complete protective equipment including chest protector, mask with throat guard, shin guards and use a proper glove. The complete safety helmet shall be required.

Chapter 9

Coaching Colt-B Pitch-T

Girls in grades 3 & 4 divisions will play Pitch-T or beginners softball. Bases are set at 60 feet. Pitching Distance: 32 feet. When the tee is brought in, the pitcher must stand at 46 foot permanent mount with at least one foot on the rubber. Circle around pitchers mound will be 8-foot radius.

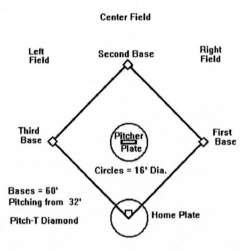

In upper league 4th grade teams may move on to straight pitch. Coaching youngsters which fall into Colt-B, should have them performing all of the basics very well. Strategy and tactics are introduced in an elemental way to the fourth graders.

As the coach, you will be required to demonstrate all of the skills that a player must acquire in order to play this game. Make sure you can get their attention whenever you show them how to do what it is you want them to do. Make it fun and use your sense of humor. Each skill has its very own way of being performed, and that is your job to teach.

Please remember that youngsters in this category have a fear of being hit by the ball. Some girls will refuse to look at the pitcher when the ball is thrown for fear of being hit. When you see this happen, don't try to force her, she must do it on her own.

In Pitch-T and straight pitch softball, the two players most likely to receive an injury are the Batter and the Pitcher. Reaction time for youngsters is slow. Next on the list of injured are the infielders from "hot" ground balls. A bad bounce can jump into a kids face and cause her to avoid getting in front of the ball to knock it down the next time a ball comes her way.

One of your worst days will be when one of your players, standing in the batting box, is caught full face by a thrown pitch. It happens, so be prepared for that eventuality. It's as bad as a line drive into your own pitcher on the mound. If you've not been a witness, at least be aware of these things happening. Kids do get hurt.

Another problem you will encounter is with the bat and batting practice. Some children forget the hazards associated with swinging the bat freely. And when one is near and they get their hands on it, they start swinging without looking to see who is around them. I feel this requires constant supervision. I've seen some nasty accidents with unsupervised bat swinging.

Teamwork and understanding the game is what should be emphasized at this level. The team must start working as a team. You are teaching where the play is to be made. You can now begin teaching the "double play", where the play "is", how to knock down the ground ball, Where the outfield play is to be made, etc..

Use your warm up drills, practice drills, and then allow base sprinting to fill in the conditioning exercise you feel they must have. For one thing you have the players moving and getting their aerobics along with an improvement in endurance. Secondly they are having fun while getting into condition.

Coaches Signals:

What you will need to do is create a simple system of hand signals to tell the batter what you want her to do at the plate. These will apply to the straight pitch players primarily. There will also be signals needed to tell the baserunners what you want them to do. If you can keep it simple the players will be able to execute and understand what you want.

Some coaches like the touch cap bill, chin, cap bill then the signal for batters in the batting box. For baserunners, the signals may avoid the cap bill and use a touch to the ear, face, arm, chest wipe and top of the cap.

It's any form of semaphore code you wish to inaugurate. The only constraint is that you be consistent. Reiterate your codes often to the players whether in a game or not. Do question and answer sessions on the codes you are using, and review before every game.

Batters Basic Signals: call for taking a pitch, swing away, bunt, sacrifice bunt and the wipe-off sign.

Baserunners Basic Signals: Go on contact and wait on base.

Signal Code Examples.

Batting Codes:

Take a pitch.	Clinched fist simulating a bat swing.
Swing away	Palm down sliding along left forearm.
Bunt	Two fingers sliding along left forearm.
Sacrifice Bunt	Wipe the belt.
Wipe off sign	Right hand wipes off chin.

Baserunners Codes:

Run of contact	Right hand pats left shoulder.
Stay option	Both hands clinched in front of body.

All we have done here is to give you some idea of what you can do and how to do it. Doing it your way is really what we want to happen for you and your team.

Player Positions

Defense in this division is played with ten players on the field. What you must do at this level of play is to select the best player for any given position and their alternates. You will be looking for certain abilities needed to give your team their best chance to win. Let's start with what is referred to as the battery, the pitcher and the catcher.

Pitcher—must be able to throw in the strike zone no less than 50% of the time. Control is more important than speed. The magic number is six out of ten in the strike zone. Attitude and poise must also play a major roll so that she may maintain her composure under pressure. The importance of ball velocity can't be overlooked and that comes with a lot of practice.

Catcher—is the workhorse of the infield. She's up and down with every pitch, throwing either back to the pitcher or to an infielder to make a play. She fields the short foul balls and foul "pop ups" at the plate. She must have great hand—eye coordination, throwing skills and catching skills.

First base—requires exceptional catching skills. She receives everything from high overhead throws to short hops. She fields grounded foul balls and "pop up" fly fouls. She must know how to position herself for the pickoff plays, and have the ability to charge the plate on a bunt. Her "head" must be in the game all of the time.

Rover—must be able to gather in or knock down the infield ground ball or handle the "pop fly" in her designated area. She is also a key player for the double play and must possess good throwing skills. She must be alert at all times, and able to backup first base, become the relay player for balls hit long to the outfield and cover first base when a bunt has pulled the first baseman to charge the infield.

Second base—must be able to gather in or knock down the infield ground ball or handle the "pop fly" in her designated area. She must be aware of how to handle the pickoff play with good catching skills. She is also a key player for the double play and must possess good throwing skills. She is also the cut-off player.

Shortstop—must be able to gather in or knock down the infield ground ball or handle the "pop fly" in her designated area. She is also a key player for the double play and must possess good throwing skills. She must be alert at all times, and able to backup second base, become the relay player for balls hit long to the outfield and cover third base when a bunt has pulled the third baseman to charge the infield.

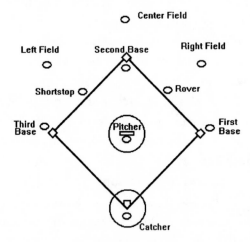

Third base—First requirement is a strong throwing arm to reach the first baseman. She must be able to charge the infield grounder and throw on the run. She's an important factor in the pickoff play and responsible on many occasions for keeping a player away from being in a scoring position. Her throwing and catching skills must be good to play the run-down plays when a baserunner is caught off base.

Left field—must possess all of the skills to backup third base. She must be alert to any play made to third from home and cover a wild throw. She must have good catching skills for the grounder, bouncer and fly ball into her area. Running speed is a big plus.

Center Field—backs up second base on every attempted put out at second. She must have excellent catching and throwing skills because she covers more territory than any other player on the team. Usually she possess excellent instincts to judge the ball coming into her realm She is a good runner. She makes the majority of outfield putouts.

Right field—backs up first base on all throws from the catcher and all balls coming into right field. She will often catch a long foul fly ball for an out. She must always be alert with good catching and throwing skills in place. She also covers any wild throws made in the pickoff play from either the catcher or pitcher.

Basic Fundamentals
Throwing the Ball.

The throwing of the ball without instruction will be somewhere between an overhand throw and sidearm. All children have their own way of throwing a ball, which simply comes naturally to them. What we want to do, is teach the overhand throwing method. If done properly, their accuracy will improve almost immediately, perhaps not in the vertical plane, but definitely in the horizontal.

The middle finger is the strongest finger of the hand and adds snap to the throw. Kinesthetically speaking, the thumb will release first and the ball will be propelled by the first, middle and third fingers. It is the forward snap of the wrist which whips these fingers forward adding velocity to the ball.

Overhand is when the throwing arm is horizontal to the ground, the elbow bent in such a way as to place the ball almost behind the head above the shoulder. The thrower turns sideways with the gloved hand towards the receiver, steps forward on that foot, twists her body as she throws and ends up facing the receiver.

If the foot she steps forward on is pointing directly towards the receiver, the balls flight should be directly at the receiver. In teaching the player how to throw, we throw "to" someplace, not "at" some place. Always emphasize "to". There are four movements involved with the throw. Arm raised and cocked with player balanced. Step towards target, rotation of hips, rotation of trunk and arm extension with a wrist snap.

Have them grasp the ball with all fingers, the most important part being with the thumb directly opposite the middle finger and under the ball. This is the basic grip for them to use. If the fingers overlay and run with the seams, the ball will appear to drop as it is in flight. If the fingers cross-over the seam, imparting backspin, the ball will appear to rise.

Catching the Ball.

This is the hardest to teach to the young players. First, they are afraid of being hit by the ball and secondly they have limited glove skills. It isn't unusual for a girl to flinch while trying to make a catch. Players must understand that this game is played through the eyes and they must watch the ball at all times. No closing the eyes or looking away from the ball.

Balls thrown below the waist can be caught with the pocket facing forward, fingers down and the free hand is used to trap the ball from falling out. From head to chest level, the pocket faces forward, thumb in, then moved to accept the ball in the pocket trapped by the free hand. The player uses it like a shield, protecting herself and grabbing the ball. Overhead balls are treated the same way with the pocket turned to face the incoming ball and trapped by the free hand.

Pitch-T Base Running.

We begin by explaining to the team that the baserunner cannot leave the base until the ball has been pitched or hit from the Tee. Each runner must be in contact at the "ready" on any base. She may stand directly on the base with her toes hooked on the edge like a starting block, or in the lead-off position with her trailing foot in contact ready to sprint.

Several conditions will quickly return her to her starting base. If the ball is hit foul. If the ball is a fly ball and caught by a fielder, she must return a quickly as possible to the safety of the base or be caught off base and get tagged out. And if the ball has been thrown to the pitcher and she has not made it halfway to the safety of her next base.

An example would be if the runner started from first base, and rounded second base heading for third base. She had just cleared second when the ball was thrown to the pitcher who now has possession. She would have to return to second base.

Pitch-T Throwing & Catching Drills.

Divide your team into two equal number of players. Place half of the team along the foul line extending just beyond first base to the outfield. Place the other half of your team on the field facing the foul line and the other players. Get at least eight feet between each player and a throwing distance of approximately 15 feet.

Each girl on the foul line is given a ball. Each girl playing must have a glove. Now, under your supervision, have them begin their throwing and catching exercise. Give plenty of attention to their throwing style, and encourage the catching effort. As the players improve, open the distance between them.

At every practice, as the girls arrive, they should pair up and start their warm-up with the throwing and catching drill. This immediately brings their focus on softball. Improvements will come in leaps and bounds at each new practice or game. This is also the pre-game warm up to get them into the spirit of things.

Catching the Infield Ground Ball

During practice and game play, the player on the field is always in the flexed or bent knee position, facing home plate, body in balance with her glove at the "ready". As the ball comes to her, she must move laterally either to her left or right to get in front of the ball. Next the glove must go down until it touches the ground, pocket facing the ball and her free hand above the glove ready to trap the ball.

The free hand does two things. It traps the ball and instantly prepares the ball to be taken and thrown, secondly it keeps the ball from bouncing out of the glove and into the players face. At times there will be a bounce, but the player can raise the glove quickly by either lifting the glove with her arm or lifting her upper body.

Catching the Infield Fly Ball

The player comes up from the flexed knee stance and must move in either of four directions; forward, backward, to the left or to the right to be in front of the ball. The glove goes up and over her head and face, pocket facing the ball. The free hand is also raised to trap the ball and give quick access for a throw. She must watch the ball all of the way into her glove.

Catching the Outfield Ground Ball.

This is the same as catching an infield grounder, but a little different in as much as it may be a bouncing ground ball. The outfielder must charge the ball, moving laterally left or right to be in the proper position to knock the ball down. If it's a roller, she scoops it up with the glove pocket facing the ball and her free hand trapping it.

If she takes it on the bounce, she catches the ball at mid body level with the pocket facing forward and the thumb pointing down. Again the free hand is used to trap, recover and throw.

Catching the Outfield Fly Ball.

The player comes up from the flexed knee stance and must move in either of four directions; forward, backward, to the left or to the right to be in front of the ball. The glove goes up and over her head and face, pocket facing the ball. The free hand is also raised to trap the ball and give quick access for a throw. She must watch the ball all of the way into her glove. Same as the infield fly ball, however when the ball is hit long, it is harder to assess where it will land.

Judging a long balls flight is difficult, especially when it is coming directly towards the outfielder. When you have a visual angle of the balls arc, it makes it easier to judge. Most errors made here are from not going back soon enough.

How to play Defense.

Get the lead runner: The goal here is to get the player in scoring position out. It can be a forced out for a runner going from second base to third base, or from first base to second base.

Infielder backup: Infielders backup throws to any base when the ball is coming from the catcher. Outfielders also backup the infielders who are working with each other. This means that every player not involved in a play should be backing up the throw.

Outfielder to relay: Is important to prevent a runner from advancing to another base. The outfielder must gather the ball and release it quickly to the relay player. The relay may be any infielder who moves out to shorten the distance from a long hit ball. More often than not, the relay player is the shortstop or rover.

Outfielder backup: All outfielders back each other up in the event a ball gets away from the outfielder in the best position to make the play. Center field may call for any ball hit to the outfield.

Pitcher's Throw: The coach will also have a signal which is given to the catcher and relayed to the pitcher. She may call for a fast ball, a change up, or whatever specialty the pitcher has.

Playing defense is teaching the team where the play is to be made. It may be to any base which will result in a runner being tagged out. It may be a combination of bases and outs. This is really the fun part of coaching, where you give them information that is as important as their playing skills. Their self esteem grows as their knowledge of the game grows.

A player may not throw as well, or bat, or run as well as another player, but when she knows where the play is, that makes her important. She feels good about herself, because she knows! And when the ball comes to her, she is confident as to what she must do. Knowledge is power. She is given the chance to make choices in the game.

We should try to keep it as basic and simple as possible for the player to grasp the game. One simple plan is, if in doubt, get the ball to the pitcher. No player may advance if the pitcher has the ball, nor may she continue to advance if the pitcher has the ball before the runner has reached the half way point between bases. Simple first rule.

Next simple rule is if no one is on base and the batter hits the ball and it is fielded, the throw should be to first base for an out. Now this is where you need a good arm on third base. What the batter will want to do is hit down the third baseline which gives her the greatest chance to reach first base. Why? Because the throw from third to first is the longest between bases. If the ball is fielded by an outfielder, the play is to second base unless fielded by right field.

Next rule will be when a runner is on first base and the batted ball is fielded by the third baseman, shortstop or second baseman to play the ball to second base. It's good for an out and holds the runner at first base. Now if your team is capable, you should coach the second baseman into throwing to first for a double play.

In the event the ball is fielded by the first baseman, you tag first and throw to the pitcher. I don't encourage throwing to second base for a double play for one reason. The runner is too vulnerable to being hit in the back by a thrown ball. I want no tears or fears. If the ball is fielded by the left fielder or center fielder, the play is to second base regardless.

Next rule will be with runners on first and second base and the batted ball is fielded by the third baseman, shortstop or second baseman to play the ball to third base. It's good for a forced out and holds the runners at first and second base. Now coach the third baseman into throwing to second base for a double play.

In the event the ball is fielded by the first baseman, you tag first and throw to the pitcher or third base. No throws to the second baseman. If the ball is fielded by an outfielder, the play is to second base regardless.

When the bases are "loaded", or a runner is on all bases, then the infielder on a ground ball tags the base closest to her and throws to the catcher at home plate. If the ball is fielded by an outfielder, depending on which outfielder and where, the throw is to the base nearest to the outfielder. The options on making the out is home, third, second and first base.

So far so good for making choices of fielded balls and where they can or should be played depending on base runners. This is a lot of stuff for youngsters to learn and be confident with, but it happens that way. And any mistakes made by their choices or lack of physical abilities is also okay. Everything is always okay, okay?

Fly-outs are another story. Every player on the field has the potential to catch a fly ball for an out. What we want to stress here to all of the players, is to keep their "heads" in the game. When a batter addresses the ball, the field must look to see where the runners are, or if there are runners on bases.

If there are no runners on any of the bases and a fly ball is caught, it is a routine out with the batter returning to the dugout. In Pitch-T, no runner can lead off from the base before the ball is thrown by the pitcher. Usually what happens with a runner, she will start the moment the ball is hit and head for the safety of the next base before the ball is caught.

If the runner has remained on base until after the ball is caught, she can then run for the next base without jeopardy of having to beat the ball back to the base she just left. If the runner has left prior to the catch, she may be put out with a throw to that base by the fielder if the ball reaches the base before the runner returns.

This is the situation we want the girls to understand and be aware of who has left a base so they can try for the second out or a double play. It happens in Pitch-T. It's the easiest way for youngsters to make a double play. Let's have an example here. If the bases were "loaded" and the short-stop caught the ball, she should immediately throw to third for an expected out. Not to second where she may hit a girl moving in her direction.

Following this further, if the second baseman caught the ball and her runner is off base, she can tag second, step inside and try for a throw to third to catch the runner who left third base. Now if the third baseman caught the ball, she tags third base, avoids throwing to second and checks first base for a possibility.

The player with the greatest number of choices in the infield is the pitcher. If she catches a fly ball, all bases are open for her to make her choice from. Her first choice should be third base to pick off a player who is considered in a scoring position. Surprisingly, the pitcher does make a lot of outs on pop flies and dribbling grounders.

The infield players have the greater opportunity for the double or the triple play than the outfielders have. An outfielder who has caught a fly ball should throw in to the base nearest to her, the other option being to throw in to the pitcher.

Defensive Drills.
Pitch-T Infield Drills.

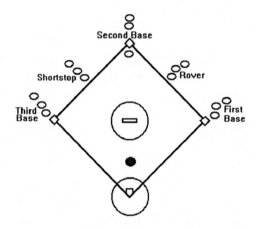

Position all of your players in the "ready" stance, slightly down with knees flexed, glove open and back straight. Instruct the infield how to move laterally and get in front of the ball to catch it.

With players & alternates at first, second, shortstop, and third base. Position yourself midway between the pitchers plate and home base. Using a bat, hit soft ground balls to any player and have that player trap and return the ball to you. Rotate to each player on the field. Encourage the player to throw the ball overhand.

If you have hit the ball to the third baseman and she has returned the ball to you, have her alternate move into position for the next ball hit to that base. Alternate all players so that all players get a chance to catch the ground ball. It is important that every player have a chance to participate in these drills.

Eventually, as the players improve, you will stand at home plate and use a bat to softly hit the ball to an infielder. The fielder must make an attempt to throw the ball home. What we are looking for at this point, is who can throw the ball the furthest. Why? We are looking for our third baseman, alternate and catcher.

Once we get the ground balls down, we work on hitting short fly balls to the infielders. "Pop flies" you might call it. From home plate begin your infield drills with grounders all around, then insert the fly balls and encourage quick get and quick throw home.

Pitch-T Outfield Drills.

With players at first, second, third base and the pitcher in the pitchers circle. Break the remaining team into three equal groups if possible. Have one group form a line at the left field position facing home in line which places them in sequence to play the fielders position. Do the same for center field and right field.

Position yourself near the pitchers circle. Bat a ground ball to left field, have the player trap the ball and return it to third base. Third base will catch the ball and throw it to the pitcher, who in turn gives it back to you. Repeat the same to center field and have the fielder trap the ball and throw to second base. Second base will catch the ball and throw it to the pitcher, who in turn gives it back to you. You repeat the same exercise with right field who returns to first base, the pitcher and back to you. Encourage the players to throw the ball overhand.

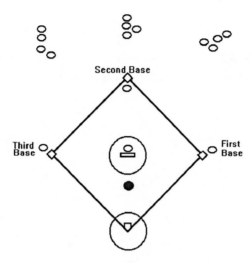

Alternate all players so that all players get a chance to catch the ground ball. It is important that every player have a chance to participate in these drills. Shift the fielding lines so that each line plays in all three outfield positions.

Position yourself near the home plate. Bat a fly ball to left field, have the player catch the ball and return it to third base. Third base will catch the ball and throw it to the pitcher, who in turn gives it back to you. Repeat the same to center field and have the fielder catch the ball and throw to second base. Second base will catch the ball and throw it to the pitcher, who in turn gives it back to you. You repeat the same exercise with right field who returns to first base, the pitcher and back to you.

Alternate all players so that all players get a chance to catch the fly ball. It is important that every player have a chance to participate in these drills. Shift the fielding lines so that each line plays in all three outfield positions.

Throwing the bases 1:

Our simplest drill will be breaking the team into four equal groups that we can assign to first base, second base, third base and home plate. The distance between each base is the same, making the drill an even challenge for each player. Starting from home plate the ball is thrown to third, from third to second, from second to first and then to home. The player at home throws to first, first throws to second, second throws to third, and third throws to home.

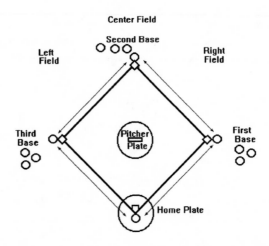

That is one circuit. Have each of the girls who participated go to the rear of her line and wait for her next time to participate. To add some fun to the throwing and catching game we begin timing how long it takes to complete the circuit. After each circuit, call out the time taken and encourage the girls to try to beat the best time recorded.

We accomplish two things here. First we get their competitiveness going and secondly we get them to focus on throwing and catching the ball. Just a little competition nulls the fear of the ball and makes each player want to do her best. For beginners, this is a lot of fun.

Throwing the bases 2:

This is somewhat like the previous exercise with the exception being the alternation of players on second and first base. Catching at second base alternates between the shortstop and the second baseman. For first base it's between the rover and the first baseman.

Assign players and alternates to each position in the infield. That will be first base, rover, second base, shortstop, third base, and catcher positions. Starting from home plate the catcher throws to third base, the third baseman throws to the shortstop on second base. The shortstop throws to first base, and the first baseman throws home to the catcher.

The catcher returns the throw to the rover on first base, the rover now throws to the second baseman on second base, the second baseman now throws to third base, and the third baseman throws home to the catcher. This is one circuit. Replace the infielders with their alternates and repeat. Run a timer on how long it takes to complete the circuit and see if the time can be improved.

Throwing the bases 3—The cut-off :

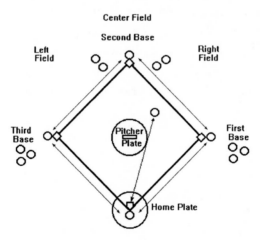

Assign players and alternates to each position in the infield. That will be first base, rover, second base, shortstop, third base, and catcher positions.

Starting from home plate the catcher throws to third base, the third baseman throws to the shortstop on second base. The shortstop throws to first base, and the first baseman throws home to the catcher.

At this point, the second baseman charges towards the pitcher's mound and the catcher throws to the second baseman. The second baseman fields the ball on the run and quickly returns the ball to the catcher.

The catcher then throws to first base, the first baseman now throws to the shortstop on second base, the shortstop in turn throws to third base, and the third baseman throws home to the catcher. This is one circuit. Replace the infielders with their alternates and repeat. Run a timer on how long it takes to complete the circuit and see if the time can be improved.

Infield Position Drill.

Assign players and alternates to each position in the infield. That will be first base, rover, second base, shortstop, third base, pitcher and catcher positions. You will take up your position at home plate to hit the ball either on the ground to the fielder, or a soft fly ball

Here's how it goes. When you hit the ball to the infielder, you call out the base where the play is to be made. If it is to the shortstop, call out for first base. The shortstop fields the ball and throws to first. First in turn now throws to the pitcher who in turn throws to the catcher, who will return it to you.

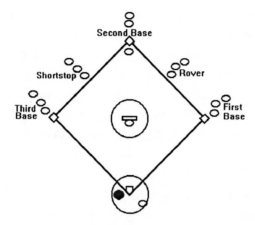

After each infielder and alternate, including the pitcher has thrown to first, make the play to second base. The second baseman follows the example set by the first baseman by returning the ball to the pitcher who in turn throws to the catcher, who will return the ball to you.

After each infielder and alternate, including the pitcher has thrown to second, make the play to third base. The third baseman follows the example set by the second baseman by returning the ball to the pitcher who in turn throws to the catcher, who will return the ball to you.

That's the drill! If you run the drill often, I would suggest that you shift players around so that each player gets a chance to play at every position. In that sense, everyone knows the difficulty of playing at any of the infield positions. And you get a better understanding of the teams weaknesses and strengths.

Infield Doubles Drill.

This drill is a little more complex than the previous drill however, it all depends on your players individual involvement and abilities. In this drill we are talking forced outs, not a fly-out and a forced out.

Assign players and alternates to each position in the infield. That will be first base, rover, second base, shortstop, third base, pitcher and catcher positions. You will take up your position at home plate to bat the ball on the ground to the fielder.

Here's how it goes. Tell the team there is a runner on first base, then you hit the ball to a fielder, calling out the base where the play is to be made. If it is to the shortstop, call out for second base. The shortstop fields the ball and throws to the second baseman who tags the base then throws to first base. First in turn now throws to the pitcher who in turn throws to the catcher, who will return it to you.

I would suggest that you shift players around so that each player gets a chance to play at every position.

Outfielders Catching Practice.

While the diamond is busy with infield practices that exclude using the outfielders, we put them to work in the outfield learning how to judge the ball coming to them.

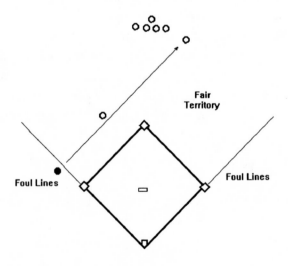

Get a coach with batting skills and position them in foul territory beyond third base. The players will go to deep mid-field. Put a relay between the batting coach and the players. After the player catches or retrieves a ball, she throws it into the relay who returns it to the batting coach.

Set your players in a line near the area you will be hitting into. Move a player into the field area you are hitting to and hit a fly ball to her. You may move her to her left, right, forward or backwards to make the play. The receiver then throws to the relay and goes to the end of the line for her next turn to catch.

Be sure to mix up the hitting so every possibility of a fly ball can be encountered. Work on having the girls turn and run away from the incoming ball when it is hit long. Run, stop, turn and check on the ball as the "go back" judgment is made. A ball is easier to catch when you come into the ball than it is when you are running backwards.

You may insert this drill when you have the field prior to a game and reap some real benefits from having the girls fresh on outfielding. Do this drill often. It works for all players, not just the outfield, so make an effort at some point to include everyone in this drill.

How to Play Offense.

Offense boils down to batting, running, observing and taking base coach's instructions. Hitting towards third base is the most basic of these simple offensive moves. It gives the runner more time to reach first base safely and it is the farthest throw an infielder can make.

You must teach the players how to take advantage of defense when situations arise such as a wild throw to the pitcher, catcher or throw to a base. The player should be ready to take the next base without having to be told by you that an opportunity has arrived.

Pitch-T begins the same as straight pitch. All player are in their respective positions on the field with a batter in the batter's box. Pitching

Distance: 32 feet. When the tee is brought in, the pitcher must stand at 46 foot permanent mount with at least one foot on the rubber. With the pitcher throwing from the mound to the catcher. It's still three strikes you're out, but no walk is granted for four balls. Instead of a walk, the batter is allowed to hit from the Tee. The Tee is place ahead of home plate, the pointed base facing the pitcher.

The player must take the proper stance inside the batting box and measure the ball height with her bat extended to the Tee. When given the signal that she can swing, it should be with all she's got. With good contact, she drops the bat inside the circle and goes for it. If the ball rolls foul of course she's called back to try again.

Batting off the Tee.

The very first thing we do is show the proper way to grip the bat and how it is swung. Indicate at what level you want the bat held in the ready position and show them how the wrists rotate as the bat is swung through it's arc. Show her how to move her body forward, shifting her weight from the back foot to the front foot as she contacts a ball

What we want to accomplish here is an understanding of how to use all of the body in hitting the ball. Most children will begin batting by using arm power only to swing the bat. Therefore, when the batter cocks up to swing, she must rotate her hips and shoulders. As her swing begins from the stance you have place her in, show her how to rotate for maximum impact.

Let's go over the steps quickly. The girl in the batter's box raises the bat, places her balance on the back foot, rotates her hip and shoulders away from the Tee. On the swing, as she shifts her weight to the front foot, twists hips, shoulders and swings the bat in an arc towards the ball. Allow the swing to follow through to her other side, then drop the bat inside the batting circle.

Set up a Tee with the batter's box outlined on the ground to show the player where to stand. Next have each player using a bat, take turns at hitting five balls off the Tee. Indicate to the player where she must stand to put the ball down the third base line, the first base line, and to center field.

Pitch-T Batting Practice on a Tee.

Using "knerf" or "woofle" balls is highly recommended in the drill for several reasons. The thin plastic skinned ball filled with holes does not have the ability to injure anyone the way a regulation ball could. It comes in all sizes, and in the same size as the recommended league ball listed under Pitch-T equipment.

Using the knerf ball removes the fear of being hit by the girls playing as fielders. You accomplish several things in this practice. Players learn to use the glove for ground and fly balls. Batters learn proper batting habits and you get a chance to evaluate the players abilities. Build their confidence with encouragement.

If you have more than one Tee, divide your players into groups based on the number of Tee's you have. Three Tee's, then you'll have three groups of equal number. Assuming you have a diamond, go to the area just beyond first base, and set your Tee's in the foul area so the ball can be batted into the fair ball area or outfield.

Batting Practice Tee

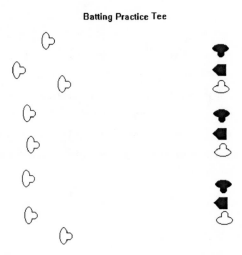

Set your Tee's twenty feet apart and assign one girl to bat at each Tee you have. Fan out the other members of the group, facing the Tee's at twenty to twenty five feet distance. A coach or assistant will work with the girls who are batting. She will Tee-up the ball and instruct the player in proper stance and batting motions.

The remainder of the group, facing the Tee's will field the balls as they are hit and throw them back to the coach at that Tee. The Tee coach is in position to encourage and instruct both the batter and the fielder. Everyone is involved in the practice. Each girl will take ten turns at bat, then exchange positions with the next batter from the field.

Batting in straight pitch.

Let's go over the batting steps quickly. The girl in the batter's box raises the bat, places her balance on the back foot, rotates her hip and shoulders away from the pitcher. On the swing, as she shifts her weight to the front foot, twists hips, shoulders and swings the bat with arms extended in an arc towards the ball. Allow the swing to follow through to her other side, then drop the bat inside the batting circle.

Straight pitch is pretty much like batting from a Tee. The big difference is explaining the strike zone and it's width and height. That is mechanically done when a Tee is used. Once she understands the strike zone and the difference between where a strike and a ball becomes defined, you are on your way. Indicate what you feel is the ideal height for her swing.

For the batter to hit a thrown ball, it takes a lot of practice. For one she must judge the speed of the ball and it's direction. Is it coming in near her or away from her? Is it to high or to low? When does she begin her swing? First rule is watch the ball all the way to the bat. If she loses sight of the ball eight feet in front of where she stands, chances are she'll miss the ball when she swings.

Batting at the Bat Cage.

This is where you have the best opportunity for teaching the batter what you want her to do and how to do it. The batter has less worry about being hit by a wild pitch than under other circumstances. You are in a position behind and to one side where you can critique each of the motions you want to see.

Selecting a cage that has a pitched ball speed in the neighborhood of fifty miles an hour should work well for 3rd and 4th graders. It can do wonders for a batter to learn to judge the speed of the ball and try to make contact. Initially we will want every girl to take a full swing at the ball. Make contact if possible. The more times you go to a bat cage, the more improvement you'll get. Familiarity breeds contact.

We usually have each girl take ten pitches, then rotate in the next batter for her turn. Continue the rotation until all batters have had an equal number of turns at bat. Not only can you instruct when the girl is in the batter's box, but also when a weaker hitter comes out of the cage. Demonstrate to her what you would like to see.

When the batters become comfortable with hitting the pitched ball, begin teaching the bunted ball. Any pitch thrown can be bunted, the only time you cannot bunt is off the Tee. Some kids pick this up very quickly and get good at it. You must show them the correct way to hold the bat, and their bunting stance.

Pitch-T Batting Practice straight pitch.

Using "knerf" or "woofle" balls is highly recommended in the drill for several reasons. The thin plastic skinned ball filled with holes does not have the ability to injure anyone the way a regulation ball could. It comes in all sizes, and in the same size as the recommended league ball listed under Pitch-T equipment.

Using the knerf ball removes the fear of being hit by the girls playing as fielders. You accomplish several things in this practice. Players learn to use the glove for ground and fly balls. Batters learn proper batting habits and you get a chance to evaluate the individual players abilities.

If you have more than one home plate, divide your players into groups based on the number of plates you have. Three plates, then you'll have three groups of equal number. Assuming you have a diamond, go to the area just beyond first base, and set your plates in the foul area so the ball can be batted into the fair ball area or outfield.

Set your plates twenty feet apart and assign one girl to bat at each plate you have. Fan out the other members of the group, facing the plates at twenty to twenty five feet distance. A coach or assistant will work with the girls who are batting. She will throw the ball and instruct the player in proper stance and batting motions.

Batting Practice

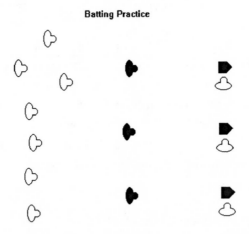

The remainder of the group, facing the batters will field the balls as they are hit and throw them back to the coach. The pitching coach is in position to encourage and instruct both the batter and the fielder. Everyone is involved in the practice. Each girl will take ten turns at bat, then exchange positions with the next batter from the field.

Pitch-T Batting Practice.

What we need here is a bushel basket of used balls that are league regulation size, and a chain link fence that borders the playing field. It doesn't sound like much, but it's necessary. What we want to do is to get the players used to hitting the regulation ball. Get the feel of how heavy it is during contact.

We will place the batter approximately six feet away and in the position of driving the ball into the fence. She will stand sideways to the fence with a coach facing her on the opposite side. The objective is to have the coach toss the ball and have the batter drive it into the fence. Now the coach is close enough to the batter, that a small arcing toss will put the ball directly in hitting position for the batter.

Batting Practice

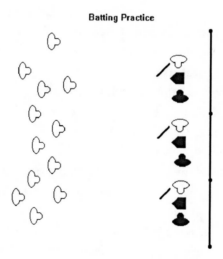

With the coach in this position, she is able to instruct the batter in her stance, her ready bat position and her follow through. Don't criticize every swing, build on the good hits that the batter makes. Every batter should take a least ten hits before being rotated. What we get from this drill is improved driving power as the body rotates through the striking motion.

Pitcher Tryouts:

Every girl on the team should be allowed to tryout for pitching on the team. You could be in for a big surprise as to who on your team can put the ball in the strike zone the highest percentage of the time. I know I've had that happen. Some coaches extend this courtesy only to a favored few. That's a mistake on a variety of levels.

I would recommend you run this tryout several times in the very beginning of the season so that each player feels she is at least given a fair chance for the opportunity to be a pitcher.

How you conduct the tryouts is simple enough. Get three hand towels which are approximately the size of the strike zone when open. You can safety pin these to the chain link fence about fifteen feet apart. Adjust their height to what would suit the average size of a girl in the batter's box. What we have is a vertical rectangle as a target.

Pace off a distance from the fence to about thirty two feet. This is where the pitcher will make her effort from. You will be working without a pitcher's plate, but that is okay. Show the girl where you want her back foot to be when she begins her windup.

Demonstrate for her the motions you want to see when she does her windup. Go through it slowly. She should square up to the home plate and begin her arm rotation. As she steps forward with her lead foot, she should release the ball. After release of the ball, the back foot should end up a shoulders width apart from the leading foot and the pitcher facing the target.

A key to throwing the ball in a straight line, is how the leading foot is placed when it contacts the ground. It should be pointing directly at the target, as the ball is pitched almost like bowling. To establish consistency, the leading foot should land in the same spot every time.

Allow each girl to throw fifteen times at the target, and count the number of hits collected. Since you are either behind or beside the girl during the throw, you are in a good position to instruct and encourage. You both are able to evaluate the pitching performance together. This is fair to both of you, as it should be.

At the conclusion of the tryouts, you can begin to select out your most promising players. Of those players with the best scores, you may wish to repeat the tryout with them only and see what the results become. This is not conclusive, but a good indicator. At least you can narrow the field of players for the pitchers position.

Pitching Target Drills.

Conduct these drills while the infield throwing drills are in progress and if some of the pitchers have alternate rolls in the infield or outfield, move them through first, and send them to their alternate positions.

Get three hand towels which are approximately the size of the strike zone when open. You can safety pin these to the chain link fence about fifteen feet apart. Adjust their height to what would suit the average size of a girl in the batter's box. What we have is a vertical rectangle as a target.

Pace off a distance from the fence to about thirty two feet. This is where the pitcher will make her effort from. You will be working without a pitcher's plate, but that is okay. Show the girl where you want her back foot to be when she begins her windup.

Demonstrate for her the motions you want to see when she does her windup. Go through it slowly. She should square up to the home plate and begin her arm rotation. As she steps forward with her lead foot, she should release the ball. After release of the ball, the back foot should end up a shoulders width apart from the leading foot and the pitcher facing the target.

Each girl will throw twenty-five times. The first ten are warm-up pitches, the next ten are for count, and the last five are for improved effort throws. Our goal is to reach a point where six out of ten pitches are in the strike zone. Consistency is what we are looking for in the beginning. Fast balls, change ups, palm balls, etc. and so forth are more advanced than we have need for here.

Pitcher & Catcher—Pitching Drill.

Conduct these drills while the infield throwing drills are in progress and if some of the pitchers have alternate rolls in the infield or outfield, move them through first, and send them to their alternate positions.

Normally we establish a pitcher/catcher practice area away from the infield practice grounds, with the dugout acting as a backstop. It can be anywhere away from the infield or outfield, and adjacent to the field fence. We do want a backstop to prevent anyone from being hit by a wild throw.

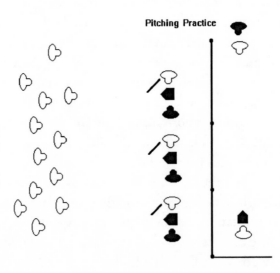

Pitching Practice

During these practice sessions, we alternate our pitchers and catchers as we go. Each pitcher will throw a total of twenty-five balls and a count will be kept. The first ten throws will be considered warm-up balls, the second ten will be for the count, and the last five as improvement of the effort. The count means we are looking for the magic number of six out of ten being in the strike zone.

The coach takes the position behind the pitcher and gives the count as the practice progresses. The catcher will be in the butt down catching position during these drills. Her job will be to stand after each catch, and return the ball 'to' the pitcher, not "at" the pitcher. This must be emphasized.

What we want first is consistency and ball control, and secondly is to get some speed on the ball. We will work on two pitches. The "fast ball" and the "change up". The pitcher must keep her body in the same fluid motion for both. It will be up to you as the coach, to make whatever adjustments are needed to the pitchers form and the catchers form.

To add fun to the drill, call "ball etc." or "strike etc." during these warm-ups. You may even play imaginary innings to add some fun to the training effort.

Pitch-T Running Drill.

Setting up to sprint from the base is the baserunners next most important thing to learn. Some runners stand over the base facing the one they will run to with their kick-off foot against the base edge for a starting block kick. The runner must watch the pitcher to throw, then jump start on the run.

Starting at home plate, line the team up for their sprint runs to the first base. On "GO", have a girl run to first, cross it and turn to her right, returning to the base. Bring up the next runner to home plate. Have the runner on first base ready to sprint to second base. On "GO" the runner on first sprints to second and the girl at home, repeats the first runners sprint to first base. All players in sequence, will run all bases until all players have completed the drill.

This can be given some variances to add fun. Assume the girl gets a double, have her rounding first and run to second, and time her effort.

You can do the same for a triple. Only you will know, so keep the times close enough so that no runner is embarrassed and build some competitive spirit.

Competition Running Drill:

This is a fun drill where two players race each other around the bases in opposite directions. Make the match-up as even as possible, then on your signal one player heads for third base and the other goes for first base. The player who headed for first base passes just inside of second base and the other player goes just outside of second base. The one to cross home plate first is the winner.

A variation on this drill is to turn it into a relay race with a softball being the baton and passed to the next runner at home plate. It is an aerobic exercise which forces the girls to develop and give a best effort in practice. Everyone is involved and having fun while gaining a level of confidence in their sprinting.

The Game Practice.

This is the old the game of "work up" baseball, once played on sand lots all over the country. It was a lot of fun for the players because you had a chance to play every position in the game.

Assign a player to every position on the field except pitcher who you become as the coach. Those not assigned will become the batting bench. The rules are quite simple. If the batter hits the ball and safely makes it to first base, well and good. However if she is put out in the process of the fielded ball reaching first before she does, she goes to the left field position and the catcher joins the batting bench.

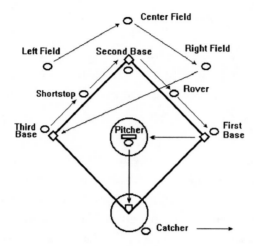

Everyone advances one position. Left field goes to center, center to right field, right field to third base, third baseman goes to shortstop, shortstop goes to second, second baseman goes to rover, rover goes to first base, first baseman goes becomes the catcher. That holds for any forced out.

A fly-out is a different story. A fly ball is hit into the infield and is caught by the shortstop. The shortstop advances to the batting bench, and the batter retires to left field. Every position behind shortstop now moves up one position. Third going to shortstop, etc.. In the event of a forced out double, everyone moves forward two positions.

In the event we have a fly-out and a forced out double. The player who caught the fly goes to the batting bench. Everyone who had a position behind the fielder who caught the fly ball, moves ahead two positions, everyone ahead of the fielder moves forward, one. The batter who hit the fly-out ends up at center field, and the forced out goes to left field.

Triples are handled in the same way to advance players towards the batting bench. Now the batting bench has it's own constraints. A player who has successfully completed three runs is retired to left field advancing all other players. This evens the playing field and continues to move the game forward.

Kids love this game, and I guess that's where the old saw comes from "out in left field." Man, he's out in left field! You'll like it also since you get a chance to do some fun coaching and become the plate umpire.

Alternate Game:

We play the same game as we have outlined above, but you play it with a softball. The pitch is a slow toss released in such a way as to pass through the strike zone for an easy hit. What we are striving for at this point is getting the batters to drive the ball in a given direction. We want the batter to attempt to hit down the third base or first base line and over second base.

Chapter 10

Ponytail Softball Playing Rules

The rules of the National Federation of High School Associations shall be enforced in the Hap Minor/Ponytail Leagues unless amended below. Situations not specifically covered in these league rules shall be left to the discretion of the Local Athletic Federation Board of Directors and Sports Office staff. (except non residents) may pitch,

Playing Rules

A. At the start of the game, each team shall designate either their coach or manager as team representative. This individual shall meet with the umpire(s) prior to game time to discuss ground rules, official starting time, etc. and shall thereafter be the only individual to enter the playing field for the purpose of necessary time-outs, rules interpretations by the game official(s) or player assistance (i.e.: injury, equipment repair, etc.). Abuse of this privilege by either coaches or managers may result in the suspension of the offending individuals and possible forfeiture of the game.

All baserunners must wear a batting helmet. Any player not doing so will be ruled out after one pitch has been delivered. If she intentionally removes her helmet while on base or advancing, she shall be called out. In addition, any runner who scores or who is put out is required to wear a batting helmet until reaching the bench/dugout while the ball is alive.

B. Baserunning rule differences for Colt B and Colt A.

    1. A runner on third, when the pitch is started, may score

        a. on a fair hit ball.

b. on a foul fly ball that is legally caught.

c. on a play on herself or any other runner.

d. if the ball is thrown to any other player except the pitcher.

e. if the pitcher does not catch the ball in the air on the return throw from the catcher. **Exception:** (Colt B: A baserunner cannot score or steal a base on a return throw or battery error from the catcher to the pitcher. A baserunner may steal second or third base when the ball leaves pitcher's hand and before the ball leaves the catcher's hand on the return throw to the pitcher. Baserunning rules pertaining to a runner on third base remain in effect).

f. on an illegal pitch.

g. on catcher's interference, if forced.

h. Base on balls. **Exception:** (Colt-B: runner may not steal or advance on Ball Four. Dead Ball. **EXCEPTION TOP COLT-B DIVISION.**)

2. Stealing home from third base shall not be permitted. A runner who is off third base illegally and has passed home plate shall be declared out by the umpire. A runner drawing a throw at home plate while attempting to acquire the right to that base illegally is considered off third base at her own risk and may be touched out before she returns safely to third base. If she touches home plate, the umpire shall declare her out.

3. Any attempt to make a play on a runner who is returning to third base after a pitched ball releases that runner from the necessity of returning to third base and permits her to score at her own risk.

4. A run may not score on a passed ball or a wild pitch. Note: A ball rebounding off the backstop and fielded by another player shall be treated the same as if the catcher had thrown the ball to the pitcher. **Exception:** (Top Colt-A Division)

5. Batter is out on dropped third strike. **Exception:** (Top Colt-A Division)

C. A practice round will precede regular play.

1. Unlimited substitution will be allowed.

D. Home team will occupy the bench near third base.

E. Pitching Distances:
1. T-Ball   pitcher will stand at 46 feet.
2. Colt B: 32 feet—When tee is brought in, pitcher will stand at 46 feet. (At least one foot on the rubber).
3. Colt A: Pitcher will stand at 35 feet
4. Yearling: Pitcher will stand at 38 feet
5. Filly: Pitcher will stand at 40 feet

F. League time limits

T-Ball: 7 innings or exactly one hour.

Colt B: 7 innings or no new inning after one hour and fifteen minutes, whichever comes first.

Colt A, Yearling, Filly: 7 innings or no new inning after one hour and thirty minutes, whichever comes first.

1. Any inning started will be completed. Exception: T-Ball
2. When more than one game is scheduled, the first game will start as listed on schedule. The second game will start as scheduled or immediately following the conclusion of the first game, whichever is later. The third game will start as scheduled or immediately following the conclusion of the second game, whichever is later.
3. When three games are scheduled, there may not be time for infield practice. Other arrangements for warm-ups should be made. (**PLEASE** use **EXTREME CAUTION** in the warm-up area).
4. **START OF GAME:** Umpire, supervisor and both team representatives will synchronize watches announce GAME TIME, NO NEW INNING AFTER! Therefore: Game time will begin, when the first girl steps into the batter's box.

G. Tie games will not be played out: Regulated number of innings or time limit, whichever occurs first.

1. Tie score will be half a win and half a loss to each team.
2. Tie games will not be played over.

H. A ten (10) run lead will constitute a radical score.

    1. Radical score games will be continued only at the request of the losing team after the following time has expired:

    Colt-B: one hour Colt-A, Yearling, Filly: one hour and fifteen minutes

    2. At a 15 run lead, the game will be continued only at the request of the winning team and losing team. However game will end when time limit has expired.

I. Forfeits:

    1. If a team knows that they cannot meet a specific date, they should inform the league in writing, **BEFORE** the schedule is run, and the league will attempt to schedule accordingly. Requests for not playing on certain dates, league, **MUST** be turned in by the last week of the practice round.

    2. There will be **ABSOLUTELY NO SCHEDULE CHANGES** after the schedule has been prepared, and the league has started. Cases involving extreme circumstances may justify canceling a game without paying a default fee, but they only may be canceled by permission of the Sports Office. Canceled games will not be made up.

    3. Teams must field a minimum of' 7 players or forfeit. The entire officials fee will be charged to the forfeiting team if the Sports Office is not notified twenty-four (24) hours ahead of time. The fee must be in the Sports Office at least 48 hours prior to the defaulting team's next game or they will forfeit the remainder of their games until the forfeit is paid.

J. T-ball, Colt-B, Colt-A: A team must play ten players when there are ten present. Yearling and Filly: A team must play nine players when nine are present.

    1. A team may start with (7) players. The line-up becomes official at game time. After game time, players who have arrived late may be added to the bottom of the line-up only, even if every batter has already batted.

2. If a team starts with ten (10) players (Yearling and Filly division; nine players), and is then forced to play with less because of injury or discipline, the game may continue with the permission of the Sports Office Supervisor. A team may never play with less than seven (7) players.

3. If a player is injured and removed from the game, she may not return even if she recovers completely.

K. Every girl must be played in every game.

1. Every girl must play in the field and come to bat. Exception: There is a possibility that a batter may not bat if her team has not batted through the line-up by game time limit.

2. Manager of opposing team violating this rule must submit a written complaint to the Sports Office within a twenty-four (24) hour period.

3. If a complaint is found valid, game will be forfeited for this violation.

4. Managers may have to substitute by time rather than innings in order to get all their girls in the game.

5. All leagues: Free substitution including hitting all the way through their players present and changing defensive players at any time must be used. (Exception: Pinch runner may be used for a sick or injured player only. The runner shall be the player who made the last out.) Any change must be cleared with the umpire and the other team manager. There is no designated hitter. Each player must play one inning per game defensively. In the event that a batter cannot take her turn at bat and continue to play due to injury or having to leave the game, her turn will be ruled an out on the first occurrence and then removed from the order for the remainder of the game. This player shall not participate further in the game. All players in attendance will appear on the line-up card and must bat in proper rotation. No change is ever permitted in the batting order. If a girl arrives late to the game, her name will be added to the bottom of the order.

Note: A pitcher who is removed from the game may re-enter the game as a pitcher. **Exception:** It states "There shall be only one charged conference between the Manager or other team representative from the dugout with each and every pitcher in an inning. The second charge conference shall result in the removal of the pitcher from the pitching position for the remainder of the game.

    6. A manager does not have to play a girl if a player needs to be disciplined for some reason. Formal notification must be given to Sports Office field supervisor and the scorekeeper before the game begins. This should be noted on scorecard and is for your protection from forfeit as in Rule K.

L. General Information

    1. Base Coaches:

        Colt-A, Yearling, Filly: a coach or a player, may coach the bases.

        T-Ball, Colt-B: a coach or a coach with a player may coach the bases.

        a. Base coach may not leave the coaching box and should not touch the runners at any time. If he/she does touch or assist the runner while a play is being made on a runner, the runner shall be declared out.

    2. Bats and equipment should be kept at first and third base ends of the dugout for safety reasons.

    3. Gloves and clothing should be kept off the dugout fence.

    4. Players must sit on the bench during the entire game. ONLY one "On-Deck" batter allowed off the bench.

    5. Managers should limit their time-outs to absolute necessity. Stalling the game will not be tolerated. If the time-out privilege is abused, we will be forced to limit the number of time-outs allowed.

    6. Courtesy runners should be used only as an "EMERGENCY" and you must obtain the opposing managers permission BEFORE doing so. Opposing managers will probably not agree to using a courtesy runner more than once for a particular batter. Runner who

is substituting can be someone who is not presently in the game. The courtesy runner will be the person who made the last out.

    7. Throwing the bat will constitute an out. Players will be warned during practice round.

M. Park Ground Rules

All ground rules will be explained by the umpires and/or park supervisor before game time. These will become the official ground rules for the game. Any situations not covered are left to the discretion of the umpire. It would be in the managers best interest to ask pertinent questions during the pre-game meeting.

IV. Equipment'

A. Each team must furnish its own equipment. All equipment should be properly marked for easy identification. Broken, or unsafe equipment should be thrown away.

B. Balls

    1. Home team will furnish a new approved ball for each league game.

    2. Visiting team will furnish a decent back-up ball.

    3. If both balls are lost, then home team will furnish a third suitable ball and visiting team the fourth, etc.

    4. Home team will have first choice of balls at the end of the game.

    5. Teams must provide decent balls during practice round.

    6. Balls are official leather 12" softball optic yellow core .47 (T-ball 10"–Colt B 11"). Non-glaze. Balls with raised seams may be used.

C. Bats

    1. Bats must be manufacturer-stamped "Official Softball" and may not be altered in any manner.

    T-Ball/Colt-B—Official Softball, Official Little League with handles taped. All bats must be equipped with a safety grip 10 inches to 18 inches in length.

D. Players must wear protective clothing at practices and games.

1. Catchers must wear a complete safety helmet, face mask with throat guard, chest protector, and shin guards.

2. It is mandatory for each batter and runner to wear a head protector. The head protector shall be type which has safety features equal to or greater than those provided by the full plastic cap with extended ear flaps which cover both ears and temples. If a batter enters the batter's box without a protective helmet, she will be declared out immediately. (This action in no way eliminates a force play situation). Any runner who scores or is put out is required to wear a batting helmet until reaching the bench/dugout while the ball is alive.

3. Teams must have their own catcher's equipment. Insurance is void if this equipment is not used at all times. Any person warming up the pitcher should wear a mask.

4. Girls warming up pitchers or any girls acting as umpire (practices) must wear mask and protector at all times.

5. All players must wear a glove or mitt; catchers and first baseman may wear mitts, all others must wear gloves.

6. All players must wear close-toed shoes. Rubber all-purpose cleats or tennis shoes are recommended. No metal-spikes or open toe shoes or sandals. Managers and coaches must also wear close-toed shoes.

7. No jewelry will be permitted during the game.

Chapter 11

Coaching Straight Pitch Players

When your players have reached the 5th grade and upwards, all games will be straight pitch. Three strikes you're out, four balls and you walk. No players are allowed to lead off of the base in preparation for running. The single most important factor will be batting. No hits, no runs.

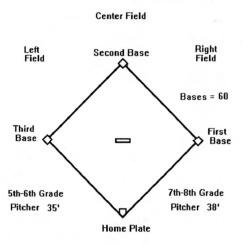

Notice that the pitcher's distance has changed from the Colt-B pitchers distance of 32'. The Colt-A pitcher is 35' and the Yearling pitcher now stands at 38'. Colt-A teams must play with ten players on the field when ten are available. Yearling must play with nine players when nine are available.

In straight pitch, during a game, two players are always under a lot of scrutiny. It's the pitcher and the catcher. They initiate everything in the game. Since that is the situation, they are under a great deal of stress to perform well. This performance pressure comes from within as well as from the outside. For these players to maintain their own composure, they require a lot of reassurance and support from you, and the rest of the team.

Give your pitcher some relief if she is not doing well, she's just in a "slump". Happens to the big time guys every year. The MLB is filled with players in "slumps". So why not these girls. Once a pitcher loses her composure and self confidence, she couldn't hit a wall with a handful of rice. If your pitcher starts to fall apart, replace her before she can lose her self esteem. Do not leave her on the mound to long and allow frustration to undo all of the efforts you have both been making.

In Colt-A we are now talking about girls from age 10 or fifth grade to girls twelve in the 6th grade. This crossover age for the players is difficult. Puberty and all the pain of hormonal changes are taking place. Temperaments and mood swings greatly effect their ability to play and have fun. The very first priority is to create the team as a team. Get camaraderie building as quickly as possible. These players need the support of each other.

One minute you're coaching a child and the next minute a quasi young teenager. You must remain supportive and always talk to the entire team when you are coaching. First rule here again is to stress teamwork and good sportsmanship during play. Accept the tremendous differences between the 5th & 6th graders in maturity, size, aggression and ability.

Your teaching methods will come up several levels as you begin their instruction in playing pick-off plays, infield and outfield drills, pitching drills, wind sprints, base sprints, etc.. Game strategies begin to enter the picture. Batting practices at a batting cage must be worked into the program. Overcoming the fear of being hit by a pitched ball in order to take a swing becomes important.

Yearlings, the girls from 7th & 8th grades are now teenagers. For the most part, these players have a lot of good skills and are ready to grow under your leadership. Again the idea of teamwork is stressed. Strategies and tactics will be the main thrust in coaching both offense and defense.

You must always treat these players with respect and not treat them as children. They are self proclaimed adults and resent any references to them as children. Some parents have trouble with this. This is the best of coaching time, the players understand exactly what you are asking them to accomplish. Their new found maturity gives these girls a sense of humor they never had before.

Your training drills will become more fun for you and the players. An emphasis must be constantly made on batting. Infield and outfield drills must be run at every practice, and the number of practices you have during a week should be no less than two. One problem you will have on infield drills will be the player side stepping a ground ball and grabbing for it backhanded. She does it to avoid being hit by the ball.

In straight pitch softball, the two players most likely to receive an injury are the Batter and the Pitcher. Next on the list of injured are the infielders from "hot" ground balls. A bad bounce can jump into a kids face and cause her to avoid getting in front of the ball to knock it down the next time a ball comes her way.

One of your worst days will be when one of your players, standing in the batting box, is caught full face by a thrown pitch. It happens, so be prepared for that eventuality. It's as bad as a line drive into your own pitcher on the mound. If you've not been a witness, at least be aware of these things happening. Kids do get hurt.

A problem you will encounter is with the bat and batting practice. Some youngsters forget the hazards associated with swinging the bat freely. And when one is near and they get their hands on it, they start swinging. often without looking to see who is around them. I feel this requires constant supervision. I've seen some nasty accidents with unsupervised bat swinging.

Coaching signals must be put in place by this time. You must be able to call for full swing or bunt, the steal, the pick-off plays, etc.. The team will play the game but you must control both defense and offense. How you do it will be up to your own creative skills. Team strength is in batting ability. No hits, no runs.

Use your warm up drills, practice drills, and then allow base sprinting to fill in the conditioning exercise you feel they must have. For one thing you have the players moving and getting their aerobics along with an improvement in endurance. Secondly they are having fun while getting into condition.

Coaches Signals:

What you will need to do is create a simple system of hand signals to tell the batter what you want her to do at the plate. There will also be signals needed to tell the baserunners what you want them to do. In the more advanced phases of the games, you will also develop signals for the catcher to relay to the pitcher. If you can keep it simple the players will be able to execute and understand what you want.

Some coaches like the touch cap bill, chin, cap bill then the signal for batters in the batting box. For the catcher's signals they use touch cap bill, nose, cap bill then the signal. For baserunners the signals may avoid the cap bill and use a touch to the ear, face, arm, chest wipe and top of the cap.

It's any form of semaphore code you wish to inaugurate. The only constraint is that you be consistent. Reiterate your codes often to the players whether in a game or not. Do question and answer sessions on the codes you are using, and review before every game.

Batters Basic Signals: call for taking a pitch, swing away, bunt, sacrifice bunt and the wipe-off sign.

Baserunners Basic Signals: Go on contact, steal, double steal, and wait on base.

Catcher/Pitcher Signals: Pickoff at first base, pickoff at second base, pickoff at third base, walk the batter, and the cut-off play. She may also call for a change up, fast ball or other specialty.

Signal Code Examples.

Batting Codes:

Take a pitch.	Clinched fist simulating a bat swing.
Swing away	Palm down sliding along left forearm.
Bunt	Two fingers sliding along left forearm.
Sacrifice Bunt	Wipe the belt.
Wipe off sign	Right hand wipes off chin.

Baserunners Codes:

Run of contact	Right hand pats left shoulder.
Stay option	Both hands clinched in front of body.
Steal	Left hand wiped down right arm.
Double steal	two hand claps.

Catcher/Pitcher Codes: This is a relay set up where you give the signal to the catcher and she relays your request to the pitcher.

Action:	Signal	Relay
Cut-off play	Touch top of cap.	Five then Five
Walk Batter	Left hand down leg wipe	Clinched fist
Fast Ball	Touch left eye	Three then one
Change up	Touch nose then ear	Three then two

All we have done here is to give you some idea of what you can do and how to do it. Doing it your way is really what we want to happen for you and your team.

Players Positions.

Defense in softball is played by nine players on the field, everyone knows that. What you must do at this level of play is to select the best player for any given position and their alternates. You will be looking for certain abilities needed to give your team their best chance to win. Let's start with what is referred to as the battery, the pitcher and the catcher.

Pitcher—must be able to throw in the strike zone no less than 50% of the time. Control is more important than speed. The magic number is six out of ten in the strike zone. Attitude and poise must also play a major roll so that she may maintain her composure under pressure. The importance of ball velocity can't be overlooked but that comes with a lot of practice.

Catcher—is the workhorse of the infield. She's up and down with every pitch, throwing either back to the pitcher or to an infielder to make a play. She fields the short foul balls and foul "pop ups" at the plate. She must have great hand—eye coordination, throwing skills and catching skills.

First base—requires exceptional catching skills. She receives everything from high overhead throws to short hops. She fields grounded foul balls and "pop up" fly fouls. She must know how to position herself for the pickoff plays, and have the ability to charge the plate on a bunt. Her "head" must be in the game all of the time.

Rover—must be able to gather in or knock down the infield ground ball or handle the "pop fly" in her designated area. She is also a key player for the double play and must possess good throwing skills. She must be alert at all times, and able to backup first base, become the relay player for balls hit long to the outfield and cover first base when a bunt has pulled the first baseman to charge the infield. (This position is for the Colt-A team set-up.)

Second base—must be able to gather in or knock down the infield ground ball or handle the "pop fly" in her designated area. She must be aware of how to handle the pickoff play with good catching skills. She is also a key player for the double play and must possess good throwing skills. She is also the cut-off player and backs up first base.

Shortstop—must be able to gather in or knock down the infield ground ball or handle the "pop fly" in her designated area. She is also a key player for the double play and must possess good throwing skills. She must be alert at all times, and able to backup second base, become the relay player for balls hit long to the outfield and cover third base when a bunt has pulled the third baseman to charge the infield.

Third base—First requirement is a strong throwing arm to reach the first baseman. She must be able to charge the infield grounder and throw on the run. She's an important factor in the pickoff play and responsible on many occasions for keeping a player away from being in a scoring position. Her throwing and catching skills must be good to play the run-down plays when a baserunner is caught off base.

Left field—must possess all of the skills to backup third base. She must be alert to any play made to third from home and cover a wild throw. She must have good catching skills for the grounder, bouncer and fly ball into her area. Running speed is a big plus.

Center Field—backs up second base on every attempted put out at second. She must have excellent catching and throwing skills because she covers more territory than any other player on the team. Usually she possess excellent instincts to judge the ball coming into her realm She is a good runner. She makes the majority of outfield putouts.

Right field—backs up first base on all bunts, throws from the catcher and all balls coming into right field. She will often catch a long foul fly ball for an out. She must always be alert with good catching and throwing skills in place. She also covers any wild throw made in the pickoff play from either the catcher or pitcher.

Basic Fundamentals
Throwing the Ball.

What we want to do, is teach the overhand throwing method. If done properly, their accuracy will improve almost immediately, perhaps not in the vertical plane, but definitely in the horizontal.

The middle finger is the strongest finger of the hand and adds snap to the throw. Kinesthetically speaking, the thumb will release first and the ball will be propelled by the first, middle and third fingers. It is the forward snap of the wrist which whips these fingers forward adding velocity to the ball.

Overhand is when the throwing arm is horizontal to the ground, the elbow bent in such a way as to place the ball almost behind the head above the shoulder. The thrower turns sideways with the gloved hand towards the receiver, steps forward on that foot, twists her body as she throws and ends up facing the receiver.

If the foot she steps forward on is pointing directly towards the receiver, the balls flight should be directly at the receiver. In teaching the player how to throw, we throw "to" someplace, not "at" some place. Always emphasize "to". There are four movements involved with the throw. Arm raised and cocked with player balanced. Step towards target, rotation of hips, rotation of trunk and arm extension with a wrist snap.

Have them grasp the ball with the first three fingers, the most important part being with the thumb directly opposite the middle finger and under the ball. This is the basic grip for them to use. If your pitchers and players have large enough hands, show them the spit finger fastball grip. If you use the split finger grip, and the fingers overlay and run with the seams, the ball will appear to drop as it is in flight. If the fingers cross-over the seam, imparting backspin, the ball will appear to rise.

Catching the Ball.

It isn't unusual for a girl to flinch while trying to make a catch. Players must understand that this game is played through the eyes and they must watch the ball at all times. No closing the eyes or looking away from the ball.

Throwing & Catching Drills.

At every practice, as the girls arrive, they should pair up and start their warm-up with the throwing and catching drill. This immediately brings their focus on softball. This is also the pre-game warm up to get them into the spirit of things.

Catching the Infield Ground Ball

During practice and game play, the player on the field is always in the flexed or bent knee position, facing home plate, body in balance with her glove at the "ready". As the ball comes to her, she must move laterally either to her left or right to get in front of the ball. Next the glove must go down until it touches the ground, pocket facing the ball and her free hand above the glove ready to trap the ball.

The free hand does two things. It traps the ball and instantly prepares the ball to be taken and thrown, secondly it keeps the ball from bouncing out of the glove and into the players face. At times there will be a bounce, but the player can raise the glove quickly by either lifting the glove with her arm or lifting her upper body.

Catching the Infield Fly Ball

The player comes up from the flexed knee stance and must move in either of four directions; forward, backward, to the left or to the right to be in front of the ball. The glove goes up and over her head and face, pocket facing the ball. The free hand is also raised to trap the ball and give quick access for a throw. She must watch the ball all of the way into her glove.

Catching the Outfield Ground Ball.

This is the same as catching an infield grounder, but a little different in as much as it may be a bouncing ground ball. The outfielder must charge the ball, moving laterally left or right to be in the proper position to knock the ball down. If it's a roller, she scoops it up with her bare hand and throws it.

If she takes it on the bounce, she catches the ball at mid body level with the pocket facing forward and the thumb pointing down. Again the free hand is used to trap, recover and throw.

Catching the Outfield Fly Ball.

The player comes up from the flexed knee stance and must move in either of four directions; forward, backward, to the left or to the right to be in front of the ball. The glove goes up and over her head and face, pocket facing the ball. The free hand is also raised to trap the ball and give quick access for a throw. She must watch the ball all of the way into her glove. Same as the infield fly ball, however when the ball is hit long, it is harder to assess where it will land.

Judging a long balls flight is difficult, especially when it is coming directly towards the player. When you have a visual angle of the balls arc, it makes it easier to judge. Most errors made here are from not going back soon enough.

How to play Defense.

Get the lead runner: The goal here is to get the player in scoring position out. It can be a forced out for a runner going from second base to third base, or from first base to second base by an infielder who is making for a double play.

Infielder backup: Infielders backup throws to any base when the ball is coming from the catcher. Outfielders also backup the infielders who are working with each other. This means that every player not involved in a play should be backing up the throw.

Outfielder to relay: Is important to prevent a runner from advancing to another base. The outfielder must gather the ball and release it quickly to the relay player. The relay may be any infielder who moves out to shorten the distance from a long hit ball. More often than not, the relay player is the shortstop.

Outfielder backup: All outfielders back each other up in the event a ball gets away from the outfielder in the best position to make the play. Center field may call for any ball hit to the outfield.

Pitcher's Pitch: The coach will also have a signal which is given to the catcher and relayed to the pitcher. She may call for a fast ball, a change up, or whatever specialty the pitcher has.

Playing defense is teaching every member of the team where the play is to be made. It may be to any base which will result in a runner being called out. It may be a combination of bases and outs. This is really the fun part of coaching, where you give them information that is as important as their playing skills. Their self esteem grows as their knowledge of the game grows.

A player may not throw as well, or bat, or run as well as another player, but when she knows where the play is, that makes her important. She feels good about herself, because she knows! And when the ball comes to her, she is confident as to what she must do. Knowledge is power. She is given the chance to make choices in the game.

One simple rule is if no one is on base and the batter hits the ball and it is fielded, the throw should be to first base for an out. Now this is where you need a good arm on third base. Why? Because the throw from third to first is the longest between bases. If the ball is fielded by an outfielder, the play is to second base unless fielded by right field.

Next rule will be when a runner is on first base and the batted ball is fielded by the third baseman, shortstop or second baseman to play the ball to second base. It's good for an out and holds the runner at first base. Now if your team is capable, you coach the second baseman into throwing to first for a double play.

In the event the ball is fielded by the first baseman, you tag first and throw to the second baseman. If the ball is fielded by the left fielder or center fielder, the play is to second base regardless.

Next rule will be with runners on first and second base and the batted ball is fielded by the third baseman, shortstop or second baseman to play the ball to third base. It's good for a forced out and holds the runners at first and second base. Now coach the third baseman into throwing to second base for a double play.

In the event the ball is fielded by the first baseman, you tag first and throw to third base. If the ball is fielded by an outfielder, the play is to second base regardless.

When the bases are "loaded", or a runner is on all bases, then the infielder on a ground ball tags the base closest to her and throws to the catcher at home plate. If the ball is fielded by an outfielder, depending on which outfielder and where, the throw is to the base nearest to the outfielder. The options on the out is home, third, second and first base.

So far so good for making choices of fielded balls and where they can or should be played depending on baserunners. These are by no means all of the possibilities that exist. And any mistakes made by their choices or lack of physical abilities is also okay. Everything is always okay, okay?

Fly-outs are another story. Every player on the field has the potential to catch a fly ball for an out. What we want to stress here to all of the players, is keeping their "heads" in the game. When a batter addresses the plate, the field must look to see where the runners are, or if there are runners on bases.

If there are no runners on any of the bases and a fly ball is caught, it is a routine out with the batter retiring to the dugout. However if you do have a runner on a base, usually she will start the moment the ball is hit and head for the safety of the next base before the ball is caught.

If the runner has left prior to the catch, she may be put out with a throw to that base by the fielder if the ball reaches the base before the runner returns. If the runner has remained on base until after the ball is caught, she can then run for the next base without jeopardy of having to beat the ball back to the base she just left.

This is the situation we want the girls to understand and be aware of who has left a base so they can try for the second out or a double play. It's the easiest way for youngsters to make a double play. Let's have an example here. If the bases were "loaded" and the shortstop caught the ball, she should immediately throw to third for an expected out. Not to second where she may hit a girl moving in her direction.

Following this further, if the second baseman caught the ball and her runner is off base, she can tag second, step inside and try for a throw to third to catch the runner who left third base. Now if the third baseman caught the ball, she tags third base, and throws to second base.

The player with the greatest number of choices in the infield is the pitcher. If she catches a fly ball, all bases are open for her to make her choice from. Her first choice should be third base to pick off a player who is considered in a scoring position. Surprisingly, the pitcher does make a lot of outs on pop flies and dribbling grounders.

The infield players have the greater opportunity for the double or the triple play than the outfielders have. An outfielder who has caught a fly ball should throw in to the base nearest to her, the other option being to throw in to the pitcher or relay player.

Defensive Drills.
Infield Drills:

Position all of your players in the "ready" stance, slightly down with knees flexed, glove open and back straight. Instruct the infield how to move laterally and get in front of the ball to catch it.

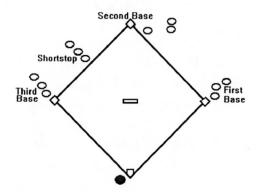

With players & alternates at first, second, shortstop, and third base. Position yourself at home plate. Using a bat, hit ground balls to any player and have that player trap and return the ball to you. Rotate to each player on the field. Encourage the player to throw the ball overhand.

If you have hit the ball to the third baseman and she has returned the ball to you, have her alternate move into position for the next ball hit to that base. Alternate all players so that all players get a chance to catch the ground ball. It is important that every player have a chance to participate in these drills.

Once we get the ground balls down, we work on hitting short fly balls to the infielders. "Pop flies" you might call it. From home plate begin your infield drills with grounders all around, then insert the fly balls and encourage quick get and quick throw home.

Outfield Drills:

With players at first, second, third base and the catcher at home plate. Break the remaining team into three equal groups if possible. Have one group form a line at the left field position facing home in line which places them in sequence to play the fielders position. Do the same for center field and right field.

Position yourself near the home plate. Bat a ground ball to left field, have the player trap the ball and return it to third base. Third base will catch the ball and throw it to the catcher, who in turn gives it back to you. Repeat the same to center field and have the fielder trap the ball and throw to second base. Second base will catch the ball and throw it to the catcher, who in turn gives it back to you. You repeat the same exercise with right field who returns to first base, the catcher and back to you.

Alternate all players so that all players get a chance to catch the ground ball. It is important that every player have a chance to participate in these drills. Shift the fielding lines so that each line plays in all three outfield positions.

Position yourself near the home plate. Bat a fly ball to left field, have the player catch the ball and return it to third base. Third base will catch the ball and throw it to the catcher, who in turn gives it back to you. Repeat the same to center field and have the fielder catch the ball and throw to second base. Second base will catch the ball and throw it to the catcher, who in turn gives it back to you. You repeat the same exercise with right field who returns to first base, the catcher and back to you.

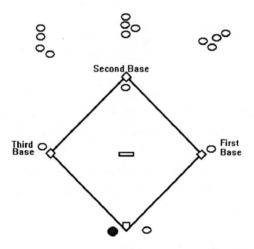

Alternate all players so that all players get a chance to catch the fly ball. It is important that every player have a chance to participate in these drills. Shift the fielding lines so that each line plays in all three outfield positions.

Throwing the bases:

Assign players and alternates to each position in the infield. That will be first base, second base, shortstop, third base, and catcher positions. Starting from home plate the catcher throws to third base, the third baseman throws to the shortstop on second base. The shortstop throws to first base, and the first baseman throws home to the catcher.

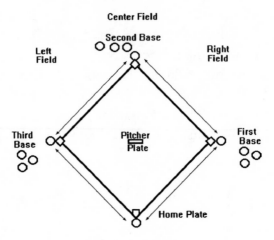

The catcher returns the throw to first base, the first baseman now throws to the second baseman on second base, the second baseman now throws to third base, and the third baseman throws home to the catcher. This is one circuit. Replace the infielders with their alternates and repeat. Run a timer on how long it takes to complete the circuit and see if the time can be improved.

Throwing the bases—The cut-off :

Assign players and alternates to each position in the infield. That will be first base, second base, shortstop, third base, and catcher positions. Starting from home plate the catcher throws to third base, the third baseman throws to the shortstop on second base. The shortstop throws to first base, and the first baseman throws home to the catcher.

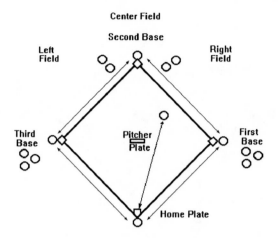

At this point, the second baseman charges towards the pitcher's mound and the catcher throws to the second baseman. The second baseman fields the ball on the run and quickly returns the ball to the catcher.

The catcher then throws to first base, the first baseman now throws to the shortstop on second base, the shortstop in turn throws to third base, and the third baseman throws home to the catcher. This is one circuit. Replace the infielders with their alternates and repeat. Run a timer on how long it takes to complete the circuit and see if the time can be improved.

Infield Position Drill.

Assign players and alternates to each position in the infield. That will be first base, second base, shortstop, third base, pitcher and catcher positions. You will take up your position at home plate to hit the ball either on the ground to the infielder, or a soft fly ball

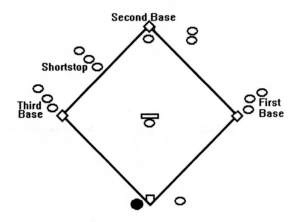

Here's how it goes. When you hit the ball to the infielder, you call out the base where the play is to be made. If it is to the shortstop, call out for first base. The shortstop fields the ball and throws to first. First in turn now throws to the pitcher who in turn throws to the catcher, who will return it to you.

After each infielder and alternate, including the pitcher has thrown to first, make the play to second base. The second baseman follows the example set by the first baseman by returning the ball to the pitcher who in turn throws to the catcher, who will return the ball to you.

After each infielder and alternate, including the pitcher has thrown to second, make the play to third base. The third baseman follows the example set by the second baseman by returning the ball to the pitcher who in turn throws to the catcher, who will return the ball to you.

That's the drill! If you run the drill often, I would suggest that you shift players around so that each player gets a chance to play at every position. In that sense, everyone knows the difficulty of playing at any of the infield positions. And you get a better understanding of the teams weaknesses and strengths.

Infield Bunting Drill.

Assign players and alternates to each position in the infield. That will be first base, second base, shortstop, third base, pitcher and catcher positions. You will take up your position at home plate to hit "Bunt" balls down the first base line, to the pitcher's mound and third base line.

All players are involved in this drill. Basemen must charge the ball and field it with their bare hand for quick throw and release to the appropriate base. The pitcher and catcher are not excluded, and must participate in the drill. What becomes crucial in this type of a drill is where the play is to be made.

What changes take place when you put the ball down the third base line? The third baseman charges the ball as the shortstop moves in to cover third base. Left field moves forward to backup the shortstop who is on third. The second baseman goes to her base backed by the center fielder moving forward. Right field moves forward to backup a throw to first base.

When the third baseman fields the ball, where is the play? That will depend on who is in a possible scoring position. The bunted ball is initiated to advance a baserunner at least one base. A sacrifice bunt is common and effective depending on the number of outs the batting team has at the time.

If you assume there is a runner on second base, you may choose to make the play to first base, then have the first baseman throw to third to hold the runner at second or try for a double out.

This works in reverse when the ball is bunted down the first base line. What changes take place when you put the ball down the first base line? The first baseman charges the ball as the second baseman moves in to cover first base. Right field moves forward to backup the second baseman who is on first. The shortstop goes to second base backed by the center fielder moving forward. Left field moves forward to backup a throw to third base.

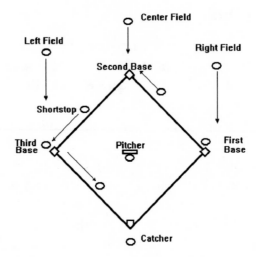

There is an option on this play with the pitcher moving to first base and having the second baseman back her up. Depending on what the circumstances may be, the pitcher is the optional backup player. While on the subject of the pitcher covering bases, let look at the situation of the wild pitch.

Any ball not knocked down by the catcher is a "get away" ball and as the catcher seeks to retrieve the ball, it is the job of the pitcher to come in and cover home plate. This is crucial when a runner is on third base with a lead off. She must also cover home plate to back up the catcher when a run down play is between third base and home.

Infield Doubles Drill.

This drill is a little more complex than the previous drill however, it all depends on your players individual involvement and abilities. In this drill we are talking forced outs, not a fly-out and a forced out.

Assign players and alternates to each position in the infield. That will be first base, second base, shortstop, third base, pitcher and catcher positions. You will take up your position at home plate to bat the ball on the ground to the fielder.

Here's how it goes. Tell the team there is a runner on first base, then you hit the ball to a fielder, calling out the base where the play is to be made. If it is to the shortstop, call out for second base. The shortstop fields the ball and throws to the second baseman who tags the base then throws to first base. First in turn now throws to the pitcher who in turn throws to the catcher, who will return it to you.

I would suggest that you shift players around so that each player gets a chance to play at every position.

Outfielders Catching Practice.

While the diamond is busy with infield practices that exclude using the outfielders, we put them to work in the outfield learning how to judge the ball coming to them.

Get a coach with batting skills and position her in foul territory beyond third base. The players will go almost to the far end of fair territory but no quite to the first base foul line marker. Put a relay between the batting coach and the players. After the player catches or retrieves a ball, she throws it into the relay who returns it to the batting coach.

Set your players in a line near the area you will be hitting into. Move a player into the field area you are hitting to and hit a fly ball to her. You may move her to her left, right, forward or backwards to make the play. The receiver then throws to the relay and goes to the end of the line for her next turn to catch.

Be sure to mix up the hitting so every possibility of a fly ball can be encountered. Work on having the girls turn and run away from the incoming ball when it is hit long. Run, stop, turn and check on the ball as the "go back" judgment is made. A ball is easier to catch when you come into the ball than it is when you are running backwards.

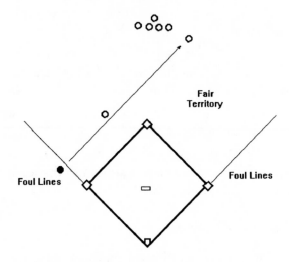

You may insert this drill when you have the field prior to a game and reap some real benefits from having the girls fresh on outfielding. Do this drill often. It works for all players, not just the outfield, so make an effort at some point to include everyone in this drill.

How to Play Offense.

Offense boils down to batting, running, observing and taking base coach's instructions. Being able to lead off a base and make the most of your opportunities.

You must teach the players how to take advantage of defense when situations arise such as a wild pitch to plate or throw to a base. The player should be ready to take the next base without having to be told by you that an opportunity has arrived

Steal a base: You watch for the pitchers windup and as it is committed, sprint for the next base. Sounds simple enough on the surface. What the baserunner must learn to do is read the pitcher's windup and hand release.

she must see the ball released. Also if the pitch is wild or gets away from the catcher sprint for the next base.

Double Steal: Is like the steal, but involves two baserunners stealing bases at the same time. Breaking in unison is confusing to the catcher who must make a choice for attempting a tag out. If you are trying to advance a player to third and your girls are on first and second, have the player on first base break first to draw the throw as the runner on second advances to third. Also used to steal home.

Sacrifice Bunt: This is used to advance a player into scoring position by laying down a bunt, with the possibility of being thrown out at first base. The coach must indicate the bunt towards third base or first base depending on how she has evaluated the quickness of the defending players.

Sacrifice fly: Used only to bring a player home from third base and a much needed score. It's tricky and only possible with very capable batters.

Take the pitch: On a three and 0 count, don't swing the bat. Take the pitch for whatever it may be. Could be a free ticket to first base.

Run on 3-2 count: If the throw is called a strike and the catcher has dropped it, you have a good chance of making first base before the play can be made against you. If it's a ball you are okay.

Run on any ball hit with 2 outs: It's a nothing to lose situation and all baserunners should take advantage of it. And most important is the player in scoring position breaking for home plate.

Batting in straight pitch.

Let's go over the batting steps quickly. The girl in the batter's box raises the bat, places her balance on the back foot, rotates her hip and shoulders away from the pitcher. On the swing, as she shifts her weight to the front foot, twists hips, shoulders and swings the bat with arms extended in an arc towards the ball. Allow the swing to follow through to her other side.

Straight pitch is pretty much like batting from a Tee. The big difference is explaining the strike zone and it's width and height. That is mechanically done when a Tee is used. Once the player understands the strike zone and the difference between where a strike and a ball becomes defined, you are on your way. Indicate what you feel is the ideal height for her swing.

For the batter to hit a thrown ball, it takes a lot of practice. For one she must judge the speed of the ball and it's direction. Is it coming in near her or away from her? Is it to high or to low? When does she begin her swing? First rule is watch the ball all the way to the bat. If she loses sight of the ball eight feet in front of where she stands, chances are he'll miss the ball when she swings.

Batting at the Bat Cage.

This is where you have the best opportunity for teaching the batter what you want her to do and how to do it. The batter has less worry about being hit by a wild pitch than under other circumstances. You are in a position behind and to one side where you can critique each of the motions you want to see.

Selecting a cage that has a pitched ball speed in the neighborhood of fifty to sixty miles an hour should work well for 5th and 6th graders. It can do wonders for a batter to learn to judge the speed of the ball and try to make contact. Initially we will want every girl to take a full swing at the ball. Make contact if possible. The more times you go to a bat cage, the more improvement you'll get. Familiarity breeds contact.

We usually have each girl take ten pitches, then rotate in the next batter for her turn. Continue the rotation until all batters have had an equal number of turns at bat. Not only can you instruct when the girl is in the batter's box, but also when a weaker hitter comes out of the cage. Demonstrate to her what you would like to see.

When the batters become comfortable with hitting the pitched ball, begin teaching the bunted ball. Any pitch thrown can be bunted. Some kids pick this up very quickly and get good at it. You must show them the correct way to hold the bat, and their bunting stance.

Batting Practice straight pitch.

Using "knerf" or "woofle" balls is highly recommended in the drill for several reasons. The thin plastic skinned ball filled with holes does not have the ability to injure anyone the way a regulation ball could. It comes in all sizes, and in the same size as the recommended league ball listed under equipment.

Using the knerf ball removes the fear of being hit by the girls playing as fielders. You accomplish several things in this practice. Players learn to use the glove for ground and fly balls. Batters learn proper batting habits and you get a chance to evaluate the individual players abilities.

If you have more than one home plate, divide your players into groups based on the number of plates you have. Three plates, then you'll have three groups of equal number. Assuming you have a diamond, go to the area just beyond first base, and set your plates in the foul area so the ball can be batted into the fair ball area or outfield.

Set your plates twenty feet apart and assign one girl to bat at each plate you have. Fan out the other members of the group, facing the plates at twenty to twenty five feet distance. A coach or assistant will work with the girls who are batting. She will throw the ball and instruct the player in proper stance and batting motions.

Batting Practice

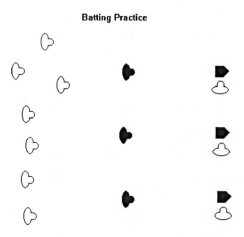

The remainder of the group, facing the batters will field the balls as they are hit and throw them back to the coach. The pitching coach is in position to encourage and instruct both the batter and the fielder. Everyone is involved in the practice. Each girl will take ten turns at bat, then exchange positions with the next batter from the field.

Batting Practice—Driving the ball.

What we need here is a bushel basket of used balls that are league regulation size, and a chain link fence that borders the playing field. It doesn't sound like much, but it's necessary. What we want to do is to get the players used to hitting the regulation ball. Get the feel of how heavy it is during contact.

We will place the batter approximately six feet away and in the position of driving the ball into the fence. She will stand sideways to the fence with a coach facing her on the opposite side. The objective is to have the coach toss the ball and have the batter drive it into the fence. Now the coach is close enough to the batter, that a small arcing toss will put the ball directly in hitting position for the batter.

Batting Practice

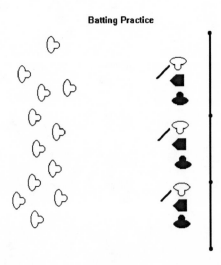

With the coach in this position, she is able to instruct the batter in her stance, her ready bat position and her follow through. Don't criticize every swing, build on the good hits that the batter makes. Every batter should take a least ten hits before being rotated. What we get from this drill is improved driving power as the body rotates through the striking motion.

Batting Practice—Directional hitting.

The intention of this drill is to teach the batter how to address the ball in the batters box. It has its roots in the T-ball approach to hitting down the baseline. The more right rotation in the batters box prior to the swing, the better your chances are to hit towards first base. It holds true for opening up the swing with left rotation towards third base.

This drill involves the entire team playing their assigned positions and rotation players as the batting team. Every player will have the opportunity to bat five balls to the left of the pitcher's mound and five balls to the right of the pitcher's mound. The infield and outfield will be returning the ball to the pitcher who throws to the catcher, who will return the ball to the assisting coach.

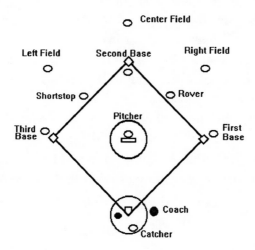

What the coach will do is toss the ball into the strike zone from the side so the batter has a chance to drive the ball in the direction she wants.

Pitcher Tryouts:

Every girl on the team should be allowed to tryout for pitching on the team. You could be in for a big surprise as to who on your team can put the ball in the strike zone the highest percentage of the time. I know I've had that happen. Some coaches extend this courtesy only to a favored few. That's a mistake on a variety of levels.

I would recommend you run this tryout several times in the very beginning of the season so that each player feels she is at least given a fair chance for the opportunity to be a pitcher. Pitching is the single most difficult part of this game. Some girls have a canny instinct when it comes to finding the correct release point of the ball.

How you conduct the tryouts is simple enough. Get three hand towels which are approximately the size of the strike zone when open. You can safety pin these to the chain link fence about fifteen feet apart. Adjust their height to what would suit the average size of a girl in the batter's box. What we have is a vertical rectangle as a target.

Pace off a distance from the fence to about thirty-five feet. This is where the pitcher will make her effort from. You will be working without a pitcher's plate, but that is okay. Show the girl where you want her back foot to be when she begins her windup. If you have 7th and 8th graders, extended the distance by three feet.

Demonstrate for her the motions you want to see when she does her windup. Go through it slowly. She should square up to the home plate and begin her arm rotation. As she steps forward with her lead foot, she should release the ball. After release of the ball, the back foot should end up a shoulders width apart from the leading foot and the pitcher facing the target.

A key to throwing the ball in a straight line, is how the leading foot is placed when it contacts the ground. It should be pointing directly at the target, as the ball is pitched almost like bowling. To establish consistency, the leading foot should land in the same spot every time.

Allow each girl to throw fifteen times at the target, and count the number of hits collected. Since you are either behind or beside the girl during the throw, you are in a good position to instruct and encourage. You both are able to evaluate the pitching performance together. This is fair to both of you, as it should be.

At the conclusion of the tryouts, you can begin to select out your most promising players. Of those players with the best scores, you may wish to repeat the tryout with them only and see what the results become. This is not conclusive, but a good indicator. At least you can narrow the field of players for the pitchers position.

Pitching Target Drills.

Conduct these drills while the infield throwing drills are in progress and if some of the pitchers have alternate rolls in the infield or outfield, move them through first, and send them to their alternate positions.

Get three hand towels which are approximately the size of the strike zone when open. You can safety pin these to the chain link fence about fifteen feet apart. Adjust their height to what would suit the average size of a girl in the batter's box. What we have is a vertical rectangle as a target.

Pace off a distance from the fence to about thirty-five feet In the Colt-A, 5th & 6th grades the pitching distance is 35 feet. In the Yearlings, 7th & 8th grades the distance is 38 feet. This is where the pitcher will make her effort from. You will be working without a pitcher's plate, but that is okay. Show the girl where you want her back foot to be when she begins her windup.

Demonstrate for her the motions you want to see when she does her windup. Go through it slowly. She should square up to the home plate and begin her arm rotation. As she steps forward with her lead foot, she should release the ball. After release of the ball, the back foot should end up a shoulders width apart from the leading foot and the pitcher facing the target.

Each girl will throw twenty-five times. The first ten are warm-up pitches, the next ten are for count, and the last five are for improved effort throws. Our goal is to reach a point where six out of ten pitches are in the strike zone. Consistency is what we are looking for in the beginning.

Fast balls, change ups, palm balls, etc. and so forth are more advanced than we have need for here. However these types of pitches are desirable to have, the pitcher should work on them at another time and place. We want meat and potatoes first.

Pitcher & Catcher—Pitching Drill.

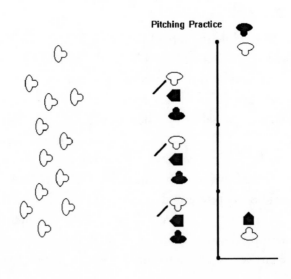

Pitching Practice

Conduct these drills while the infield throwing drills are in progress and if some of the pitchers have alternate rolls in the infield or outfield, move them through first, and send them to their alternate positions.

Normally we establish a pitcher/catcher practice area away from the infield practice grounds, with the dugout acting as a backstop. It can be anywhere away from the infield or outfield, and adjacent to the field fence. We do want a backstop to prevent anyone from being hit by a wild throw.

During these practice sessions, we alternate our pitchers and catchers as we go. Each pitcher will throw a total of twenty-five balls and a count will be kept. The first ten throws will be considered warm-up balls, the second ten will be for the count, and the last five as improvement of the effort. The count means we are looking for the magic number of six out of ten being in the strike zone.

During these practices you must always remind the pitcher to keep the catcher in the game. Uncontrolled pitches that hit the dirt in front of home plate are not allowed. Enforce the "over the plate" rule with every pitcher. If she is good enough to get five or six out of ten over the plate, her "wild pitch" percentage should drop considerably.

The coach takes the position behind the pitcher and gives the count as the practice progresses. The catcher will be in the butt down catching position during these drills. Her job will be to stand after each catch, and return the ball 'to' the pitcher, not "at" the pitcher. This must be emphasized.

What we want first is consistency and ball control, and secondly is to get some speed on the ball. We will work on two pitches. The "fast ball" and the "change up". The pitcher must keep her body in the same fluid motion for both. It will be up to you as the coach, to make whatever adjustments are needed to the pitchers form and the catchers form.

To add fun to the drill, go through all of the motions that the plate umpire goes through during a game. Call "ball etc." or "strike etc." during these warm-ups. You may even play imaginary innings to add some fun to the training effort.

Catcher's Drill.

During the pitching drill, we will want to instruct the catcher to keep her bare hand behind her back or leg to protect it. The glove should do the work with its deep pocket and the catchers ability to squeeze the ball when received. How the glove faces the pitcher as a target is emphasized.

The catcher has two positions; butt down where her entire body is a shield against a bad pitch and blocks the ball from getting away during a short hop throw. Butt up is when her upper body is parallel to the ground and she is in a crouching position. This position is often taken when the catcher is anticipating having to throw to a base for a pickoff play.

When runners are on bases, the catcher must be butt up to get the ball away as quickly as possible. This is a difficult position to catch from but it is necessary to get that extra part of a second in order to make the play.

So butt down or butt up must be worked into the pitching and catching drill. The catcher is the hardest worked player on the team and must be able to rifle a ball all the way to second base.

Running Drill.

Starting at home plate, line the team up for their sprint runs to the first base. On "GO", have a girl run to first, cross it and turn to her right, returning to the base. Bring up the next runner to home plate. Have the runner on first base ready to sprint to second base. On "GO" the runner on first sprints to second and the girl at home, repeats the first runners sprint to first base. All players in sequence, will run all bases until all players have completed the drill.

This can be given some variances to add fun. Assume the girl gets a double, have her rounding first and run to second, and time her effort. You can do the same for a triple. Only you will know, so keep the times close enough so that no runner is embarrassed and build some competitive spirit.

What you've gained for yourself is a knowledge of who has the quickness for a steal or double steals. Who is most likely to be able to get a double and who should you hold on second base instead of trying for a triple. Can the batter on a bunt make it to first, and is the runner on third fast enough to score on a bunt.

Competition Running Drill:

This is a fun drill where two players race each other around the bases in opposite directions. Make the match-up as even as possible, then on your signal one player heads for third base and the other goes for first base. The player who headed for first base passes just inside of second base and the other player goes just outside of second base. The one to cross home plate first is the winner.

A variation on this drill is to turn it into a relay race with a softball being the baton and passed to the next runner at home plate. It is an aerobic exercise which forces the girls to develop and give a best effort in practice. Everyone is involved and having fun while gaining a level of confidence in their sprinting.

Lead off base Drill:

Taking a lead off of a base is done when the pitcher has committed to a throw and released the ball. The ball may be hit or caught and the runner has gained several steps in the direction of the base that the runner wants to obtain. This is an anticipation move by the baserunner which can unnerve the catcher.

The basic question for every player is how far away from the base must I be? Rule of thumb is two sprint steps and a dive from the base. A dive? Yes a dive to the base. First the dive is a body length and the players position is low enough to most likely miss a tag. If done well, the worst thing that happens is a dirty shirt.

Initially, have each player at first base go through the two step and dive exercise. Rotate the line through the drill several times and look for the players that have difficulty with reaching the bag. If a problem, shorten the distance for that particular player.

When and how does a player know when to dive for the base? By watching the ball to see if it is hit fair or foul. Let's review the rules for the baserunner.

1. A runner on third, when the pitch is started, may score

   a. on a fair hit ball.

   b. on a foul fly ball that is legally caught.

   c. on a play on herself or any other runner.

   d. if the ball is thrown to any other player except the pitcher.

   e. if the pitcher does not catch the ball in the air on the return throw from the catcher. **Exception:** (Colt B: A baserunner cannot score or steal a base on a return throw or battery error from the catcher to the pitcher. A baserunner may steal second or third base when the ball leaves pitcher's hand and before the ball leaves the catcher's hand on the return throw to the pitcher. Baserunning rules pertaining to a runner on third base remain in effect).

   f. on an illegal pitch.

   g. on catcher's interference, if forced.

   h. Base on balls. **Exception:** (Colt B: runner may not steal or advance on Ball Four. Dead Ball. **Exception top COLT B division.**)

2. Stealing home from third base shall not be permitted. A runner who is off third base illegally and has passed home plate shall be declared out by the umpire. A runner drawing a throw at home plate while attempting to acquire the right to that base illegally is considered off third base at her own risk and may be touched out before she returns safely to third base. If she touches home plate, the umpire shall declare her out.

3. Any attempt to make a play on a runner who is returning to third base after a pitched ball releases that runner from the necessity of returning to third base and permits her to score at her own risk.

4. A run may not score on a passed ball or a wild pitch. **Note:** A ball rebounding off the backstop and fielded by another player shall be treated the same as if the catcher had thrown the ball to the pitcher. **Exception:** (Top Colt A Division)

5. Batter is out on dropped third strike. **Exception:** (Top Colt A Division)

The exercise calls for you, the coach to be on the pitcher's mound and a runner at first base. Set up like the pitcher, coming up on balance, then with your leading foot moving forward simulate a throw. The condition of the exercise is, if you move your leading foot in the direction of home plate, have the runner take a lead towards second base.

Rotate the players through the exercise several times and see how many can be caught in a mistake. This is an important running drill and should be done often enough to keep the players aware of the importance of leading off the base.

The Game Practice.

This is the old the game of "work up" baseball, once played on sand lots all over the country. It was a lot of fun for the players because you had a chance to play every position in the game.

Assign a player to every position on the field except pitcher who you become as the coach. Those not assigned will become the batting bench. The rules are quite simple. If the batter hits the ball and safely makes it to first base, well and good. However if she is put out in the process of the fielded ball reaching first before she does, she goes to the left field position and the catcher joins the batting bench.

Everyone advances one position. Left field goes to center, center to right field, right field to third base, third baseman goes to shortstop, shortstop goes to second, second baseman goes to first base, first baseman goes becomes the catcher. That holds for any forced out.

A fly-out is a different story. A fly ball is hit into the infield and is caught by the shortstop. The shortstop advances to the batting bench, and the batter retires to left field. Every position behind shortstop now moves up one position. Third going to shortstop, etc.. In the event of a forced out double, everyone moves forward two positions.

In the event we have a fly-out and a forced out double. The player who caught the fly goes to the batting bench. Everyone who had a position behind the fielder who caught the fly ball, moves ahead two positions, everyone ahead of the fielder moves forward, one. The batter who hit the fly-out ends up at center field, and the forced out goes to left field.

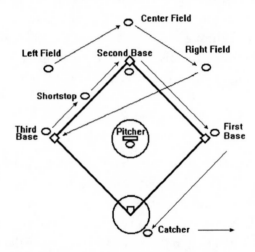

Triples are handled in the same way to advance players towards the batting bench. Now the batting bench has it's own constraints. A player who has successfully completed three runs is retired to left field advancing all other players. This evens the playing field and continues to move the game forward.

Kids love this game, and I guess that's where the old saw comes from "out in left field." Man, he's out in left field! You'll like it also since you get a chance to do some fun coaching and become the plate umpire

Alternate Game:

We play the same game as we have outlined above, but you play it with a softball. The pitch is a slow toss released in such a way as to pass through the strike zone for an easy hit. What we are striving for at this point is getting the batters to drive the ball in a given direction. We want the batter to attempt to hit down the third base or first base line and over second base.

Chapter 12

Practice Schedule planning.

It all begins with the amount of time allocated to the sports program by either the school, YWCA, Youth Foundation, Parks and Recreations Sport Office, Inner City Athletics, etc.. Depending on the categories of your players, you may be given a game schedule from eight to twelve or more weeks.

This begins a string of questions you will have to deal with. What is the amount of time allowed for a practice session, and how many sessions may you have per week? How much practice will there be prior to your first game? Considering the age and ability of your team and its players, how much can you reasonably accomplish before your first game?

How do you start planning your practices? That is based upon the facilities available to you and their times of availability. It is also based upon the availability of your team members. It can't be during school hours, so it must be after school. Most of the softball diamonds will be closed to practice on the weekends because that is normally when they will schedule games. However you do have a preseason period which may change some of those restrictions in your favor.

I suggest that you plan your practices right after school or during the early evening. Avoid late evening practices if possible. Schedule your practice time on any day Monday through Friday. For some of you, there may be Sunday practices if facilities are available. If no park diamonds are available, you may be able to use the ones at your local schools.

If you are coaching very young players, the earlier in the evening the better for them. There is also the consideration of when the parents are able to bring the kids to practice. In formulating the practice schedule you have to take into account all of the factors which comprise the team as a whole. That is the availability of yourself, the players and the parents along with the facility.

Use a practice game among your team players and attempt to assess their weakness' and their strengths. Based upon your observation you are now able to determine the type of instruction to be given. For the most part, your younger players will require the greatest amount of time in the basics.

When you prioritize the players needs in training, be realistic. Keep an honest perspective of what can and cannot be achieved with a limited amount of practice and training time. Refrain from having expectations that are beyond the abilities of the kids. Don't be intimidated by the game schedule. Set a steady learning pace for the team and let the win or loss of a game become secondary.

Make a chart. The left hand side or column represents your time frame. On the right side place the exercises or drills you want to have the players practice. As you progress with your training program, you will begin removing some of the earlier exercises and replacing them with new ones. Follow your plan. Obtain your teams training goals and their success.

As a general example, let's assume we can have a one hour practice session once or twice a week. How do you make something happen during such a short period of time? We start by breaking down the one hour into segments.

Allow the first ten minutes to be their throwing and catching warm up drills. For the youngest of players, set the throwing distance at about 15 feet. Half way through, increase the distance by 5 feet. With older players, start at approximately the distance from home plate to the pitchers mound, then move them back equivalent to the distance between bases.

Take the next thirty minutes for infield and outfield instructions on where the play is made depending on having a man on base. Do your infield throwing drills and outfield catching and throwing drills.

Take the next ten to fifteen minutes for batting practice.

Take the remainder of your time for game practice allowing the kids to have fun with the game. A coach will do the pitching during this period of play.

In **Category I**, which is T-Ball—K, 1st and 2nd grades.

At this age level what we are doing is teaching the very basics of the game and allowing the children to have fun. I would also recommend that you have a booster session at games end, pointing out the many good things that the children were able to do.

The basics you are teaching is throwing, catching, batting, running and position assignments. With infield positions, assign alternate players to them. Assign alternates as well for the outfield positions. The idea being that any girl can play any position if necessary.

The previous general outline applies here quiet well. One thing you will want to emphasize is how and where to stand in the batters box when addressing the ball on the tee. If this becomes part of the practice game, make sure the batter wears a helmet and that the pitcher also wears a helmet. Closely instruct on not throwing the bat.

In the **Category II** Colt-B, which is third and fourth grade playing Pitch-T softball. Schedule in at least a one hour or more practice session per week. Normally these youngsters will be scheduled for their games on a Saturday. The best hours for children in this group is before seven p.m..

If you are scheduled for a Saturday game, arrange your practice on either Wednesday, Thursday or Friday. I shouldn't have to tell you that, but I going to anyway and the reasons are obvious. More of the practice session will be retained and used by the players than if they have had a longer layoff. The fresher the practice session, the better the game. The better they play, the better they feel and the better job you are doing.

In Pitch-T you must consider scheduling in pitching practices for your designated pitchers and catchers. Have assistant coaches help in the catching category. You still follow the general schedule outline we have already covered, now you refine it with instructional pitching.

Pitch-T is a two element game wherein we still use the Tee to hit from and the second is where no Tee is used. The straight pitch game is normally for upper league of 4th grade players. One thing that must be taught in your baserunning practice is that no one can leave the base until the pitcher releases the ball or the ball is hit.

Schedule visits to a batting cage to introduce your players to batting a live ball. This is where and how you can improve their performance at the batting box.

Category III Colt A, is a whole new ball game for these kids. We now have 5th and 6th grade players. No more Tee's to work from, it's all pitch softball now. Going to a bat cage cannot be ignored, it's an absolute must do thing. You should schedule an entire session just for that.

I suggest that you schedule at least two practice sessions a week regardless of the games played. You will have practice and league games which will be split between Saturdays and week nights. The practice session should be one hour or more if possible.

Allow the first ten minutes to be their throwing and catching warm up drills. With players at this age, start at approximately the distance from home plate to the pitchers mound, then move them back equivalent to the distance between bases.

Take the next thirty minutes for infield and outfield instructions on where the play is made depending on having a player on base. Do your infield throwing drills and outfield catching and throwing drills. Begin the anticipation jump starts getting off the base techniques with a dive return. Review coaching signals and the pickoff plays.

Work in your pitching drills during this period.

Take the next ten to fifteen minutes for batting practice.

Take the remainder of your time for game practice allowing the kids to have fun with the game. A coach will do the pitching during this period of play.

Schedule visits to a batting cage to introduce your players to batting a live ball. This is where and how you can improve their performance at the batting box. Instruct them in the advantages of being either at the front of the box towards the pitcher or at the back of the box to compensate for the incoming balls height above ground.

These players are capable of performing all of the basics pretty well. Your guide lines will be more detailed and directed than in the previous practice session. You should be teaching them your set of control signals you will be using during a game.

Category IV is Yearlings, a new step up for everyone involved. 7th & 8th grades players are big strong girls. They throw hard, bat long and play the game very well. Batting is the key to these players game.

Schedule visits to a batting cage for your players to improve batting a live ball. This is where and how you can improve their performance at the batting box. Instruct them in the advantages of being either at the front of the box towards the pitcher or at the back of the box to compensate for the incoming balls height above ground.

This is where hustle begins and just playing ends. I suggest that you schedule at least two practice sessions a week regardless of the games played. You will have practice and league games which will be split between Saturdays and week nights. The practice session should be no less than one hour and more if possible.

Allow the first ten minutes to be their throwing and catching warm up drills. With older players, start at approximately the distance from home plate to the pitchers mound, then move them back equivalent to the distance between bases.

Take the next thirty minutes for infield and outfield instructions on where the play is made depending on having a player on base. Do your infield drills and outfield drills. Begin the anticipation jump starts getting off the base techniques with a dive return. Review coaching signals and the pickoff plays.

Take the next ten to fifteen minutes for batting practice.
Work in your pitching drills during this period.

Take the remainder of your time for game practice allowing the kids to have fun with the game. A coach will do the pitching during this period of play.

Schedule visits to a batting cage to improve your players at batting a live ball. This is where and how you can improve their performance at the batting box.

Players in this age group have a strong tendency to emulate the other players on the team who are better players and learn from them. They quickly pick up from each other, so that you don't have to concentrate on the basics as you must with the younger players. They are also more interested in helping each other become better. As a result, your better players will always help the less skilled players to improve without you making a point of it.

Chapter 13

Warm up drills

The warm up drills are intended to exercise the body in such a way as to compliment the practice drills. Muscles and ligaments used during play should be stretched and warmed before active drills are run. What we are interested in here is the ham string, Achilles tendon, lower back and upper shoulders.

Those drills listed below are only a few of the many possibilities now available to you. Employ as many other or different ones as you are familiar with, and use them judiciously. Categories I & II require the most gentle exercises. Beyond those categories expand freely, but do not turn an exercise into an ordeal.

Circuit Jogging—Warm-up No. 1.

This is not a race. Slow jog the perimeter of the infield, shaking out the arms and hands. This is intended to be a loosening up jog. Get the blood flowing and the entire body warmed up. The number of circuits will depend on the children's ages and conditions. Don't make it an ordeal, it's just a simple warm-up that you can start or finish with.

Waist, Torso & Upper Body—Warm-up No. 2.

Form the players into two lines that face you from left to right and two players deep. Have them spread out sideways until their fingers cannot touch.

Have them spread their feet shoulder width facing you. On the first count with arms extended at shoulder height sideways, have them twist their torso to face their upper bodies to the left.

Second count returns them to facing you, the third count have them twist their torso to face their upper bodies to the right. Fourth count returns them to facing forward again. Do twelve cycles.

Waist, Torso & Upper Body—Warm-up No. 3.

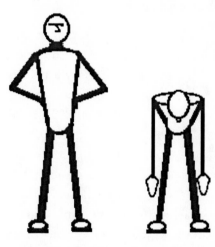

Form the players into two lines that face you from left to right and two players deep. Have them spread out sideways until their fingers cannot touch. Have them spread their feet shoulder width facing you. On the first count with hands on their hips, have them bend forward and reach for their toes.

Second count returns them upright to facing you, on the third count have them bend their upper bodies backwards. Fourth count returns them to upright facing forward again. Do twelve cycles.

Vertical Body Stretch and Calf—Warm-up No. 4.

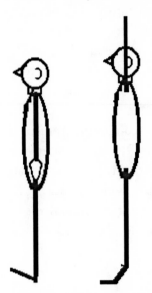

Form the players into two lines that face you from left to right and two players deep. Have them spread out sideways until their fingers cannot touch. Have them spread their feet slightly apart and hands at their sides facing you.

On the first count rock backwards on the heels while lifting the toes from the ground. Second count rocks them forward onto their toes and up as they raise their hands and arms reaching for the sky. The third count returns them to their starting position. Do twelve cycles.

Vertical Body Stretch and Side—Warm-up No. 5.

Form the players into two lines that face you from left to right and two players deep. Have them spread out sideways until their fingers cannot touch. Have them spread their feet shoulder width and hands on their hips facing you.

On the first count raise their left hand reaching for the sky and bending to their right side. Second count returns them to the start position. Third count raise their right hand reaching for the sky and bending to their left side. Fourth count returns them to the start position. Do twelve cycles.

Leg Lunge and Quadriceps—Warm-up No. 6.

Form the players into three lines. Each line will follow the person at the head of the line. With their back straight, step forward with the right foot, plant the foot and lower the body until the left knee touches the ground. Hold a moment then push back to the up position and pull the left foot even with the right.

With their back straight, step forward with the left foot, plant the foot and lower the body until the right knee touches the ground. Hold a moment then push back to the up position and pull the right foot even with the left.

Continue the exercise until the players have crossed the width of the diamond. This is not a hurry up exercise, take your time. Some of the small players may have difficulty, if so, shorten the length of the training path.

Leg Squats and Quadriceps—Warm-up No. 7.

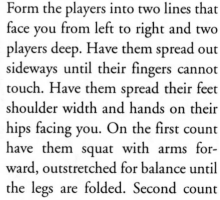

Form the players into two lines that face you from left to right and two players deep. Have them spread out sideways until their fingers cannot touch. Have them spread their feet shoulder width and hands on their hips facing you. On the first count have them squat with arms forward, outstretched for balance until the legs are folded. Second count returns them to their original position. Do twelve cycles.

Side Straddle Hop—Warm-up No. 8.

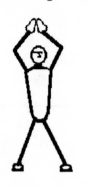

Form the players into two lines that face you from left to right and two players deep. Have them spread out sideways until their fingers cannot touch. Have them place their feet together and hands at their sides facing you. On the count of one, they must jump vertically, spreading their feet and raising their hands overhead to clap. On the second count they return to their starting position. You may use a two count or four count cadence.

Vertical Jump—Warm-up No. 9.

Form the players into two lines that face you from left to right and two players deep. Have them spread out sideways until their fingers cannot touch. What we want is to have the players jump as high with arms going up on the jump as they can reach. The cadence is jump, bounce, bounce, jump, bounce, bounce. The bounce is a short vertical jump above ankle high.

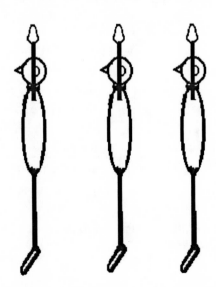

Biography

An engineer, writer and author. Life long sports fan and for more than thirty years a volunteer coach in sports. During this period of time I have also shown new coaches how to plan, schedule and rotate their players during games. Teaching how to coax the best from players without pushing the player.

0-595-24179-4

Printed in the United States
107119LV00005B/312/A